COMMANDS OF THE NEW TESTAMENT

BOOKS BY KEVIN M. THOMAS

Commands of the New Testament
Living the Life of Proverbs
Why Daughters Need Their Dads
The Happiest Women
Chinese Spiritual Thoughts
The Great Path
Wisdom and Virtue
Tao Te Ching Decoded

COMMANDS OF THE NEW TESTAMENT

God's Guide for Your Life

KEVIN M. THOMAS

COMMANDS OF THE NEW TESTAMENT
God's Guide for Your Life

Copyright © 2024 by Kevin M. Thomas

All rights reserved. No part of this book may be reproduced or transmitted in any form or by any means, electronic or mechanical, including photocopying, recording, or by any storage or retrieval system without permission in writing from the copyright author.

For more information, address to KETNA Publishing P.O. Box 90861, Burton, Michigan, 48509

First KETNA Printing Edition 2024

Cover Design by Libzyyy
Book Interior and E-book Design by Amit Dey (amitdey2528@gmail.com)

Bible Verses are public domain from the World English Bible and are used with permission from WEB and Michael Johnson.

is a registered trademark of KETNA Publishing

Printed in the US

Library of Congress Control Number: 2024915970

ISBN: 978-1-948265-08-9 (soft cover)
ISBN 978-1-948265-09-6 (hard cover)
ISBN 978-1-948265-10-2(e-book)

DEDICATION

I dedicate this book to you and all those seeking a deeper, more fulfilling relationship with God, Jesus, and the Holy Spirit. May it help you gain a more profound knowledge of God's word and bring you many blessings.

And remember; "Owe no one anything, except to love one another; for he who loves his neighbor has fulfilled the law." Romans 13:8

ACKNOWLEDGMENTS

Putting a book together goes beyond my writing. It incorporates proofreading, formatting, cover design, and a collaborative effort and I thank my long time contributors. I would also like to thank Michael Johnson and the World English Bible for contributing most of the bible verses between the Matthew and Revelation sections. So, I thank all of those who contributed to this effort to bring you a final product that I believe will bring you closer to God, to have a deeper understanding of our incredible savior, Jesus, and deeper fulfillment from the Holy Spirit that guides us and therefore, helps me and our team deliver to you what I believe are the wishes of God and a guide for your life. Also understand, these Commands are just one part of Christian understanding. There is the Old Testament and the New Testament in their entirety, as well as what God communicates to each person via the Holy Spirit. Therefore, I thank God for allowing me to share his wonderful words of truth.

TABLE OF CONTENTS

Introduction Xxxv
Section One: Books of the New Testament. 1
Section Two: Commands of the New Testament Revelation
to Revelation. 5

THE COMMANDS OF MATTHEW. 7

1. Turn From Your Sins 9
2. Obey God, Follow Jesus. 10
3. Be Glad When You Are Persecuted 11
4. Let Your Good Deeds Shine. 11
5. Jesus Came to Fulfill the Law and Commandments . . . 11
6. Settle Your Differences 12
7. Avoid Sins and Vows 13
8. Do Not Resist Those That Hurt You 14
9. Give to Others 15
10. Love Your Enemies 15
11. Strive to Be Perfect 15
12. Do Your Good Deeds in Private 16

13. Pray in Private. ... 17
14. Follow This Example of Prayer ... 17
15. Fast in Private. ... 18
16. Store Your Treasures in Heaven. ... 19
17. Don't Worry About Clothes, Food, or Drink ... 19
18. Do Not Judge. ... 20
19. Do Unto Others ... 21
20. Follow Jesus. ... 22
21. Show Mercy. ... 22
22. Discipleship Guidelines ... 23
23. Jesus Gives Rest. ... 27
24. A Tree Identifies the Fruit. ... 28
25. Plant Seeds ... 28
26. Honor Your Mother and Father. ... 29
27. Take Up Your Cross and Follow Jesus ... 30

THE COMMANDS OF MARK. ... 31

1. Repent of Your Sins. ... 33
2. Follow Jesus. ... 33
3. Plant Seeds ... 34
4. Discipleship. ... 34
5. Listen to Jesus. ... 36
6. Take Up Your Cross and Follow Jesus ... 36

7. Be A Servant to Everyone 37
8. Don't Tolerate Sin in Yourself. 38
9. Be Like Children 39
10. Remember the Ten Commandments 40
11. Sell Your Possessions, Give to the Poor, and Follow Jesus. 40
12. Believe and Receive 40
13. Forgive 41
14. Give to God and Give to the Government 41
15. Love God With All Your Heart 42
16. Love Others 42
17. Beware of Scribes 42
18. Don't Be Misled By False Teachers 43
19. Endure All Trials and Be Saved 43
20. No One Knows When Jesus Will Return 47
21. Keep Watch. 47
22. Remember the Body and Blood of Jesus. 48
23. Go Into the World and Preach the Gospel 49

THE COMMANDS OF LUKE **51**
1. Prove That You Have Repented 53
2. Give to the Poor. 54
3. Don't Extort Money. 54

4. Serve God 54
5. Fish For Men's Souls 55
6. Love Your Enemies 56
7. Don't Be A Hypocrite 58
8. Plant Seeds 58
9. Discipleship Travel 59
10. Follow Jesus 60
11. The Harvest Is Great 60
12. Love Your God With All Your Heart 62
13. Show Mercy 63
14. How You Should Pray 63
15. Keep Seeking 63
16. Give to the Poor 64
17. Beware of Pharisees 64
18. Don't Be Afraid 65
19. Guard Against Greed 66
20. Don't Worry About Food and Clothes 66
21. Sell Your Possessions 67
22. Wait For His Return 67
23. Settle Your Differences Before Going to Court ... 68
24. Work Hard to Enter God's Kingdom 68
25. Be Humble, Invite the Poor 69
26. Use Worldly Resources to Benefit Others 71

27. Rebuke Sin 71
28. Follow Jesus, Don't Look Back 72
29. Keep Asking. 72
30. Be Like Children 73
31. Remember the Commandments 73
32. Give to Caesar, Give to God. 73
33. Beware of Teachers of the Law 74
34. Keep Watch For the Return of Jesus 74
35. God Will Answer Through You 75
36. The Kingdom of God Is Near 76
37. Remember His Body and Blood. 77
38. The Greatest Are Servants 78

THE COMMANDS OF JOHN 79

1. Follow Jesus. 81
2. The Father's House Is Not A Marketplace. 81
3. You Must Be Born Again 82
4. Human Souls Are Ready For Harvesting 82
5. Stop Sinning 83
6. Working On the Sabbath 84
7. Trust in the Light 85
8. Wash Each Other's Feet. 86
9. Trust in God, Trust in Jesus 86
10. Live in Jesus, Love Each Other 87

xvi   Commands of the New Testament

11. Ask, and You Will Receive 88
12. Be A Disciple 89
13. Receive the Holy Spirit 89
14. Feed His Sheep 90
15. As For You, Follow Jesus 91

THE COMMANDS OF ACTS 93

16. Repent of Your Sins and Be Baptized 95
17. Repent of Your Sins .95
18. Repent of Wickedness 96
19. If God Calls It Clean, Don't Call It Impure 96
20. Preach Everywhere 97
21. Don't Mock the Truth 97
22. Abstaining 98
23. Feed God's People 99
24. Beware of False Teachers 99

THE COMMANDS OF ROMANS **101**

1. Don't Serve Sin 103
2. Do Not Brag (The Gentiles Blessing) 104
3. Be A New Person 105
4. Measure Yourself By Faith 106
5. Use Your God-Given Gifts 106
6. Love People 107

7. Work Hard 107
8. Be Patient 107
9. Help God's Children 107
10. Bless the Persecutors 108
11. How to Treat Others 108
12. Obey the Authorities and Laws 109
13. Love Your Neighbor 110
14. Put On the Shining Armor of Right Living 111
15. Live Decent Lives 111
16. Accept Others 112
17. Eating Guidelines 112
18. Accept Different Christian Beliefs 112
19. Help Others 114
20. Greet Each Other 115
21. Avoid Divisions 115

THE COMMANDS OF I CORINTHIANS **117**
1. Live in Harmony 119
2. Understand True Wisdom (Become A Fool) 120
3. Don't Boast 120
4. Don't Judge 120
5. Cast Out Evil 121
6. Who to Judge 122
7. Handling Legal Disputes 123

8. Run From Sin 123
9. Marriage and Sex 124
10. Circumcision 126
11. Do God's Work 126
12. Slaves Don't Worry 126
13. Be Free From Pride and Fear 127
14. Marriage and Divorce 127
15. Avoid Distractions 128
16. Unmarried Benefits 128
17. Eating Conscience 130
18. Run to Win 131
19. Avoid Idolatry 131
20. Avoid Sexual Immorality 131
21. Don't Test God 132
22. Think of Others 132
23. Food Offered to Idols 132
24. Do All For God 133
25. Head Coverings 134
26. Partake in My Body 135
27. Partake in My Blood 135
28. Desire Godly Gifts 136
29. Make Love Your Highest Goal and Ask For Special Abilities 136

30. Tongues Require Interpretation 137
31. Plan No Evil 137
32. Strengthen Each Other 137
33. Speaking in Tongues 137
34. Speaking in Prophesy 138
35. Women Silent in the Church 138
36. Avoid Bad Company 139
37. Stop Sinning 139
38. Work Enthusiastically For the Lord 140
39. Money Collection (Tithing) 140
40. Stand Firm 141
41. Show Kindness and Love 141

THE COMMANDS OF 2 CORINTHIANS 143

1. Open Your Heart to Salvation 145
2. Don't Team With Wickedness 146
3. Cleanse Yourself 146
4. Open Your Hearts to the Truth 147
5. Give What You Can 147
6. Be A Cheerful Giver 148
7. Only Boast of the Lord 148
8. Listen 148
9. Pass the Test of Genuine Faith 149

THE COMMANDS OF GALATIANS 151
   1. Love Your Neighbor. 153
   2. Let the Holy Spirit Guide Your Life 154
   3. Avoid Being Conceited or Jealous 154
   4. Guide People Back to the Path 155
   5. Share Each Other's Troubles and Problems 155
   6. Do Your Very Best At Your Work 155
   7. Pay Those Who Teach You the Word 156
   8. You Reap What You Sow 156
   9. Do What Is Right and Good 156

THE COMMANDS OF EPHESIANS 157
   1. Remember Your Past 159
   2. Stop Sinning 160
   3. Become A New Person 160
   4. Stop Lying 161
   5. Don't Let Anger Control You 161
   6. Stop Stealing 161
   7. Don't Use Abusive Language 161
   8. Follow God in Everything. 162
   9. Avoid Immorality and Foolish Talk 163
  10. Don't Excuse Sins 163
  11. Live in the Light. 164
  12. No Drunkenness 164

13. Sing Songs to God 165
14. Give Thanks to God 165
15. Submit to One Another 165
16. Obey Your Parents 167
17. Raise Children With Loving Discipline 167
18. Slaves and Slave Owners 167
19. Put On God's Armor 168

THE COMMANDS OF PHILIPPIANS 171

1. Live As A Citizen of Heaven 173
2. Don't Be Intimidated By Your Enemies 173
3. Encourage Each Other 174
4. Be Humble 174
5. Live Like Jesus. 175
6. Work Hard 175
7. Don't Argue 176
8. Hold Firmly to the Word 176
9. Be Glad in the Lord 176
10. Circumcision 177
11. Be A Mature Christian 177
12. Stay True to the Lord 178
13. Be Full of Joy 178
14. Be Unselfish 178
15. Don't Worry 178

16. Focus On What Is True and Pure. 179

THE COMMANDS OF COLOSSIANS **181**
   1. Follow Jesus. 183
   2. Avoid Human Thinking. 183
   3. Focus On Heaven 184
   4. Deaden Yourself to Sin 185
   5. Get Rid of Anger 185
   6. Don't Lie 185
   7. Be Kind 186
   8. Forgive 186
   9. Love. 186
 10. Live in Peace 186
 11. Be Wise, Sing to God 187
 12. Represent Jesus 187
 13. Wives Submit 187
 14. Husbands Submit 187
 15. Children Obey 188
 16. Use Fair Discipline 188
 17. Slaves Obey 188
 18. Work Hard 188
 19. Slave Owners 189
 20. Pray. 189
 21. Share the Good News 189

| 22. Conversation Should Be Gracious. 190
| 23. Carry Out the Ministry 190

THE COMMANDS OF 1 THESSALONIANS. 191

  1. Avoid Sexual Sin 193
  2. Live A Quiet Life 194
  3. Stay Alert 194
  4. Encourage Each Other 195
  5. Encourage the Lazy, Frightened and Weak 195
  6. Don't Repay Evil 196
  7. Be Joyful 196
  8. Always Pray 196
  9. Be Thankful. 196
10. Don't Smother the Holy Spirit 196
11. Don't Scoff At Prophecies. 197
12. Test Everything 197
13. Stay Away From Evil 197
14. Greet With A Kiss. 197
15. Read This Letter. 197

THE COMMANDS OF 2 THESSALONIANS. 199

  1. God Provides Rest. 201
  2. Don't Be Fooled By the Day of the Lord's Arrival. . . 202
  3. Stand Firm to the Truth. 202

4. Pray For the Lord's Message. 203
5. Stay Away From Lazy Believers 203

THE COMMANDS OF 1 TIMOTHY 205
1. Don't Waste Time in Meaningless Discussion. 207
2. Be Filled With Love 208
3. Fight Well in the Lord's Battles 208
4. Cling Tightly to Your Faith 208
5. Pray For the People 209
6. Pray With Hands Lifted. 209
7. Women Dress Appropriately 209
8. Women Don't Teach Men 210
9. Elder/Pastor Requirements 210
10. Don't Waste Time Arguing 212
11. Be An Example 213
12. Read Scripture to the Church 213
13. Use Your Spiritual Gifts. 213
14. Be Task Focused 213
15. Watch How You Live 213
16. Treat Older Men Well 214
17. Treat Older Women Well. 214
18. Take Care of Widows 214
19. Widows As Church Workers 215
20. Elders Should Be Paid Well 216

21. Elder Discipline. 216
22. Show No Favoritism 217
23. Wine For Medicine 217
24. Slaves Show Full Respect 217
25. Wholesome Teaching Promotes Godly Life 218
26. Be Wary of Godless Teaching 219
27. Be Content With Food and Clothing 219
28. Money Is the Root of All Evil 219
29. Run From Evil 220
30. Fight the Good Fight For Eternal Life. 220
31. Obey Commands Without Wavering 221
32. Trust in God, Not Money 221
33. Avoid Foolish Discussions. 222

THE COMMANDS OF 2 TIMOTHY 223

1. Be Strong and Bold 225
2. Never Be Ashamed of the Lord 225
3. Hold Onto Truthful Teaching 226
4. Guard the Truth 226
5. Be Strong With Grace. 226
6. Teach Great Truths 226
7. Endure Suffering 227
8. Farmers Enjoy First Fruit 227
9. Preach the Good News 227

10. Stop Fighting Over Words 227
11. Work Hard 228
12. Avoid Foolish Talk 228
13. Turn From Evil 228
14. Run From Lust and Evil Thoughts 229
15. Run From Arguments 229
16. Be Gentle and Kind 229
17. Gently Instruct Those Who Oppose the Truth 229
18. Stay Away From Scoffers 230
19. Remain Faithful to the Teaching 231
20. Preach the Word, in Season or Out 231
21. Carry Out the Ministry 231

THE COMMANDS OF TITUS 233

22. Elder Requirements 235
23. Silence Those Who Refuse to Obey 236
24. Promote Right Living 237
25. Older Men Requirements 237
26. Older Women Requirements 237
27. Younger Women Requirements 237
28. Younger Men Requirements 238
29. Be An Example For Others 238
30. Slave Requirements 238
31. Obey the Government 239

32. Avoid Slander 239
33. Be Devoted to Good Deeds 239
34. Avoid Quarrels Over Theological Ideas 240
35. Warn Divisive People 240
36. Help With the Urgent Needs of Others 241

THE COMMANDS OF PHILEMON **243**

THE COMMANDS OF HEBREWS **247**
1. Don't Turn From God 249
2. Focus On Entering the Place of Rest 250
3. Become Mature in Understanding 251
4. Follow God's Examples 251
5. Fully Trust God 252
6. Hold Onto Salvation 252
7. Motivate Others to Love and Kindness 252
8. Meet Together 253
9. Keep Your Trust in the Lord 253
10. It's Impossible to Please God Without Faith 253
11. Strip Off Sin and Run Your Race For God 254
12. Keep Your Eyes On Jesus 254
13. Accept the Lord's Discipline 255
14. Follow the Straight Path 255
15. Listen and Obey 256

16. Love Each Other 257
17. Don't Love Money 257
18. Follow the Example of Those Who Teach the Word . . 258
19. Avoid Strange Ideas 258
20. Be A Sacrifice For God 258
21. Obey Spiritual Leaders and Pray For Them 259

THE COMMANDS OF JAMES 261

1. Consider Troubles A Joy 263
2. Be Patient 263
3. Seek Wisdom 263
4. God Honors the Poor 264
5. God Humbles the Rich 264
6. God Never Tempts You to Do Wrong 265
7. Be Quick to Listen, Slow to Speak, Slow to Anger . . 265
8. Get Rid of All Evil 265
9. Be A Doer of the Word 266
10. Don't Favor Some People Over Others 266
11. Remember, the Poor Inherit
    The Kingdom of God 266
12. Watch What You Say and Do 267
13. Church Teachers Are Judged Strictly 267
14. Avoid Blessing and Curses From the Same Mouth . . 268
15. Live Honorably and Do Good Works 268

16. Avoid Jealousy and Selfishness. 268
17. Resist the Devil, and He Will Flee 268
18. Come Closer to God, and He Comes Closer to You . 269
19. Divided Loyalty Leads to Sorrow 269
20. Don't Criticize and Judge Others 269
21. Seek What the Lord Wants 270
22. The Rich Will Weep and Groan. 270
23. Be Patient and Wait For the Lord's Return 271
24. Do Not Swear or Take An Oath 271
25. Pray During Hardships 272
26. Anoint the Sick With Oil and Pray 272
27. Confess Your Sins to Each Other 272

THE COMMANDS OF 1 PETER **273**

1. Use Self-Control 275
2. Be Obedient. 275
3. Be Holy. 276
4. You Are Judged On What You Do 276
5. Remember God Paid to Save You. 276
6. Cleanse Your Sins By Obeying the Truth 277
7. Get Rid of Hatred. 277
8. Crave Pure Spiritual Milk 277
9. Avoid Worldly Desires 278
10. Behave Well Around Unbelievers 278

11. Submit to Authority 278
12. Respect Everyone 279
13. Slaves Submit to Masters 279
14. Wives Accept Your Husbands Plans 279
15. Focus On the Beauty Within 280
16. Husbands, Honor Your Wives 280
17. Be of One Mind 280
18. Don't Retaliate 281
19. Hold Your Tongue 281
20. God Will Reward You If You Suffer and Do Right . . 282
21. Worship Jesus and Share Your Faith 282
22. Do What Is Right 282
23. Sin Loses Its Power When You Suffer For Jesus 283
24. Be Anxious to Do the Will of God 283
25. Be Disciplined Men of Prayer 283
26. Show Deep Love For Each Other 284
27. Share Your Home 284
28. Use Your Special Gifts 284
29. Be Glad in Suffering For Jesus 285
30. Feed God's Flock 286
31. Lead By Example 286
32. Young Men Should Accept Elder Authority 286
33. Be Humble 287

34. Give Your Worries to God 287
35. Stay Alert to the Devil and Stand Firm 287
36. Greet Each Other With A Kiss 287

THE COMMANDS OF 2 PETER **289**
37. 2 Peter 291
38. Have Moral Excellence 291
39. Have Self-Control 291
40. Share Brotherly Affection 291
41. Work Hard 292
42. Remember the Commands of Jesus 292
43. Be Patient; A Day Is Like A Thousand Years to
    The Lord 293
44. Live A Peaceful Life 293
45. Don't Be Fooled By Wicked People 293
46. Grow in Spiritual Knowledge 293

THE COMMANDS OF 1 JOHN **295**
1. Don't Love This Evil World 297
2. Stay Faithful to Teaching 297
3. Remain in Fellowship With Jesus 298
4. Do What Is Right 298
5. Stay the Course If the World Hates You 298
6. Show Compassion 298
7. Love Each Other 299

xxxii Commands of the New Testament

   8. Believe in Jesus and Love One Another 299
   9. Stay Away From False Prophets 299
10. Be Loving and Kind. 300
11. Those Who Love God Must Love Other Believers. . . 300
12. Pray For Sinners. 300
13. Stay Away From Anything That Replaces God 301

THE COMMANDS OF 2 JOHN 303

   1. Love One Another 305
   2. Love Is Doing What God Commanded Us to Do. . . 305
   3. Beware of False Teachers 306

THE COMMANDS OF 3 JOHN 307

   1. Support Teachers and Missionaries 309
   2. Follow What Is Good 309

THE COMMANDS OF JUDE 311

   1. Defend the Faith and Truth. 313
   2. Remember the Apostle's Predictions. 313
   3. Build Each Other Up in Faith. 314
   4. Await the Mercy of Jesus 314
   5. Show Mercy to Those With Wavering Faith. 314
   6. Be Merciful to Sinners While Hating Sin 315

THE COMMANDS OF REVELATION 317

   1. Repent and Do the Works You Did Before 319

   2. Be Victorious and Be Given Fruit From the Tree Of Life 319

   3. Remain Faithful and Receive the Crown 320

   4. Be Victorious and Avoid the Second Death 320

   5. Repent of Your Sin 321

   6. Be Victorious and Receive Manna and A New Name . 321

   7. Hold Tightly to What You Have 321

   8. Listen to the Spirit 321

   9. Strengthen Your Actions and Deeds. 322

  10. Repent or Be Punished 322

  11. Listen to the Spirit 322

  12. Hold On So No One Can Take Your Crown 323

  13. Turn From Indifference and Become Enthusiastic . . 323

  14. Solve the Puzzle of the Beast 323

  15. Worship God 324

  16. Harmful or Vile, Righteous or Holy, Let It Continue . 324

  17. Come and Drink From the Water of Life 325

Section Three: Characteristics of New Testament Believers . 327

Section Four: Condensed Character Traits of the New Testament Christian 365

Section Five: Simple Steps to Following God **381**

Section Six: Helpful Prayers to Turn Your Life Over to God. **385**

Section Seven: Growing in Jesus Christ Daily **389**

About the Author. **393**

Book Summary **395**

About Ketna Publishing **397**

INTRODUCTION

This book incorporates the books of the New Testament. While we become saved by grace and remember Jesus shed his blood on the cross to take away our sins, God has expressed through his words that obeying his commands is vital to having a relationship with him. "If you love me, you will obey my Commandments." (John 14:15)

This book was written to help guide your life while remembering that proper understanding comes from reading the entire Bible, including the Old Testament. Therefore, I encourage you to read the ENTIRE Bible continually and to meditate on God's word. Also, remember that God speaks to our hearts. So, learning and understanding what God wants for our lives will come from many sources. Still, the New Testament is a solid foundation of what you need to know in building the relationship with God you desire and that God desires from you.

SECTION ONE

BOOKS OF THE NEW TESTAMENT

NEW TESTAMENT BOOKS

1. Matthew
2. Mark
3. Luke
4. John
5. Acts
6. Romans
7. 1 Corinthians
8. 2 Corinthians
9. Galatians
10. Ephesians
11. Philippians
12. Colossians
13. 1 Thessalonians
14. 2 Thessalonians

15. 1 Timothy
16. 2 Timothy
17. Titus
18. Philemon
19. Hebrews
20. James
21. 1 Peter
22. 2 Peter
23. 1 John
24. 2 John
25. 3 John
26. Jude
27. Revelation

SECTION TWO

COMMANDS OF THE NEW TESTAMENT REVELATION TO REVELATION

THE COMMANDS OF MATTHEW

MATTHEW

MATTHEW CHAPTER 3

TURN FROM YOUR SINS

2 "Repent, for the Kingdom of Heaven is at hand!"

8 "Therefore produce fruit worthy of repentance!"

NOTE: To repent means to turn from wrong action and sin. Fruit of the spirit includes love, joy, peace, kindness, goodness, faithfulness, gentleness, self-control, and forbearance (Patience or leniency).

MATTHEW CHAPTER 4

OBEY GOD, FOLLOW JESUS

4 But he answered, "It is written, 'Man shall not live by bread alone, but by every word that proceeds out of God's mouth.'"

7 Jesus said to him, "Again, it is written, 'You shall not test the Lord, your God.'"

10 Then Jesus said to him, "Get behind me, Satan! For it is written, 'You shall worship the Lord your God, and you shall serve him only.'"

17 From that time, Jesus began to preach, and to say, "Repent! For the Kingdom of Heaven is at hand."

19 He said to them, "Come after me, and I will make you fishers for men."

NOTE: Satan tempts us with possessions and physical needs but when tempted, we must turn to God and focus on Heaven.

MATTHEW CHAPTER 5

BE GLAD WHEN YOU ARE PERSECUTED

12 "Rejoice, and be exceedingly glad, for great is your reward in heaven. For that is how they persecuted the prophets who were before you."

LET YOUR GOOD DEEDS SHINE

16 "Even so, let your light shine before men, that they may see your good works and glorify your Father who is in heaven."

JESUS CAME TO FULFILL THE LAW AND COMMANDMENTS

17 "Don't think that I came to destroy the law or the prophets. I didn't come to destroy, but to fulfill.

18 For most certainly, I tell you, until heaven and earth pass away, not even one smallest letter or one tiny pen stroke shall in any way pass away from the law, until all things are accomplished.

19 Therefore, whoever shall break one of these least commandments and teach others to do so, shall be called least in the Kingdom of Heaven; but whoever shall do and teach them shall be called great in the Kingdom of Heaven."

NOTE: Jesus did not speak against the laws of God but against the way people were mistreated by religious leaders' application of them. Things like the Ten Commandments are very applicable today.

SETTLE YOUR DIFFERENCES

23 "If therefore you are offering your gift at the altar, and there remember that your brother has anything against you,

24 ...leave your gift there before the altar, and go your way. First be reconciled to your brother, and then come and offer your gift.

25 Agree with your adversary quickly while you are with him on the way; lest perhaps the prosecutor deliver you to the judge, and the judge deliver you to the officer, and you be cast into prison.

26 Most certainly I tell you, you shall by no means get out of there until you have paid the last penny."

NOTE: Try to settle your differences before going to court, and even if it is not a legal dispute, try to reason together.

AVOID SINS AND VOWS

29 "If your right eye causes you to stumble, pluck it out and throw it away from you. For it is more profitable for you that one of your members should perish than for your whole body to be cast into Gehenna.

30 If your right hand causes you to stumble, cut it off, and throw it away from you. For it is more profitable for you that one of your members should perish, than for your whole body to be cast into Gehenna."

33 "Again you have heard that it was said to the ancient ones, 'You shall not make false vows, but shall perform to the Lord your vows,'

34 but I tell you, don't swear at all: neither by heaven, for it is the throne of God;

35 nor by the earth, for it is the footstool of his feet; nor by Jerusalem, for it is the city of the great King.

36 Neither shall you swear by your head, for you can't make one hair white or black.

37 But let your 'Yes' be 'Yes' and your 'No' be 'No.' Whatever is more than these is of the evil one."

NOTE: Gehenna was a smoldering garbage dump outside of Jerusalem and referred to as a place of misery.

DO NOT RESIST THOSE THAT HURT YOU

39 "But I tell you, don't resist him who is evil; but whoever strikes you on your right cheek, turn to him the other also.

40 If anyone sues you to take away your coat, let him have your cloak also.

41 Whoever compels you to go one mile, go with him two."

NOTE: It's a fantastic testimony to love those who hate you.

GIVE TO OTHERS

42 "Give to him who asks you, and don't turn away him who desires to borrow from you."

LOVE YOUR ENEMIES

44 "But I tell you, love your enemies, bless those who curse you, do good to those who hate you, and pray for those who mistreat you and persecute you…"

STRIVE TO BE PERFECT

48 "Therefore you shall be perfect, just as your Father in heaven is perfect."

MATTHEW CHAPTER 6

DO YOUR GOOD DEEDS IN PRIVATE

1 "Be careful that you don't do your charitable giving before men, to be seen by them, or else you have no reward from your Father who is in heaven.

2 Therefore, when you do merciful deeds, don't sound a trumpet before yourself, as the hypocrites do in the synagogues and in the streets, that they may get glory from men. Most certainly I tell you, they have received their reward.

3 But when you do merciful deeds, don't let your left hand know what your right hand does,

4 so that your merciful deeds may be in secret, then your Father who sees in secret will reward you openly."

NOTE: This is a reminder our giving must be pure and not for the appearance of doing good things for others.

PRAY IN PRIVATE

5 "When you pray, you shall not be as the hypocrites, for they love to stand and pray in the synagogues and in the corners of the streets, that they may be seen by men. Most certainly, I tell you, they have received their reward.

6 But you, when you pray, enter into your inner room, and having shut your door, pray to your Father who is in secret; and your Father who sees in secret will reward you openly.

7 In praying, don't use vain repetitions as the Gentiles do; for they think that they will be heard for their much speaking.

8 Therefore don't be like them, for your Father knows what things you need before you ask him."

NOTE: While public prayer is acceptable, that prayer's motivation is what matters.

FOLLOW THIS EXAMPLE OF PRAYER

9 Pray like this:" 'Our Father in heaven, may your name be kept holy.

10 Let your Kingdom come. Let your will be done on earth as it is in heaven.

11 Give us today our daily bread.

12 Forgive us our debts, as we also forgive our debtors.

13 Bring us not into temptation, but deliver us from the evil one. For yours is the Kingdom, the power, and the glory forever. Amen.'"

FAST IN PRIVATE

16 "Moreover when you fast, don't be like the hypocrites, with sad faces. For they disfigure their faces that they may be seen by men to be fasting. Most certainly I tell you, they have received their reward.

17 But you, when you fast, anoint your head and wash your face,

18 so that you are not seen by men to be fasting, but by your Father who is in secret; and your Father, who sees in secret, will reward you."

NOTE: Again, make sure your fasting is pure and not hypocritical.

STORE YOUR TREASURES IN HEAVEN

19 "Don't lay up treasures for yourselves on the earth, where moth and rust consume, and where thieves break through and steal;

20 but lay up for yourselves treasures in heaven, where neither moth nor rust consume, and where thieves don't break through and steal;

21 for where your treasure is, there your heart will be also."

NOTE: Fulfilling God's obedience and seeking to please him helps us understand he has more in store for us while remembering that earthly possessions are temporary.

DON'T WORRY ABOUT CLOTHES, FOOD, OR DRINK

25 "Therefore I tell you, don't be anxious for your life: what you will eat, or what you will drink; nor yet for your body, what you will wear. Isn't life more than food, and the body more than clothing?

28 Why are you anxious about clothing? Consider the lilies of the field, how they grow. They don't toil, neither do they spin…"

31 "Therefore don't be anxious, saying, 'What will we eat?', 'What will we drink?' or, 'With what will we be clothed?'"

33 "But seek first God's Kingdom and his righteousness; and all these things will be given to you as well.

34 Therefore don't be anxious for tomorrow, for tomorrow will be anxious for itself. Each day's own evil is sufficient."

MATTHEW CHAPTER 7

DO NOT JUDGE

1 "Don't judge, so that you won't be judged."

5 "You hypocrite! First remove the beam out of your own eye, and then you can see clearly to remove the speck out of your brother's eye."

6 "Don't give that which is holy to the dogs, neither throw your pearls before the pigs, lest perhaps they trample them under their feet, and turn and tear you to pieces."

7 "Ask, and it will be given you. Seek, and you will find. Knock, and it will be opened for you."

NOTE: In terms of dogs and pigs, we should share the word with unbelievers but discern how much time we should spend on this with people who won't listen or who are unclean.

DO UNTO OTHERS

12 "Therefore, whatever you desire for men to do to you, you shall also do to them; for this is the law and the prophets."

13 "Enter in by the narrow gate; for the gate is wide and the way is broad that leads to destruction, and there are many who enter in by it."

15 "Beware of false prophets, who come to you in sheep's clothing, but inwardly are ravening wolves."

MATTHEW CHAPTER 8

FOLLOW JESUS

22 But Jesus said to him, "Follow me, and leave the dead to bury their own dead."

NOTE: Jesus wants you to follow him without hesitation.

MATTHEW CHAPTER 9

SHOW MERCY

2 Behold, they brought to him a man who was paralyzed, lying on a bed. Jesus, seeing their faith, said to the paralytic, "Son, cheer up! Your sins are forgiven you."

13 "But you go and learn what this means: 'I desire mercy, and not sacrifice, 'for I came not to call the righteous, but sinners to repentance."

22 But Jesus, turning around and seeing her, said, "Daughter, cheer up! Your faith has made you well." And the woman was made well from that hour.

38 "Pray therefore that the Lord of the harvest will send out laborers into his harvest."

NOTE: We see that faith (in verses 2 and 38) can heal our bodies so we can do God's work. God wants people to share the good news with others to fulfill his purpose.

MATTHEW CHAPTER 10

DISCIPLESHIP GUIDELINES

7 "As you go, preach, saying, 'The Kingdom of Heaven is at hand!'

8 Heal the sick, cleanse the lepers, and cast out demons. Freely you received, so freely give.

9 Don't take any gold, silver, or brass in your money belts.

10 Take no bag for your journey, neither two coats, nor sandals, nor staff: for the laborer is worthy of his food.

11 Into whatever city or village you enter, find out who in it is worthy, and stay there until you go on.

12 As you enter into the household, greet it…

13 If the household is worthy, let your peace come on it, but if it isn't worthy, let your peace return to you.

14 Whoever doesn't receive you or hear your words, as you go out of that house or that city, shake the dust off your feet.

15 Most certainly I tell you, it will be more tolerable for the land of Sodom and Gomorrah in the day of judgment than for that city."

16 "Behold, I send you out as sheep among wolves. Therefore be wise as serpents and harmless as doves.

17 But beware of men, for they will deliver you up to councils, and in their synagogues they will scourge you.

18 Yes, and you will be brought before governors and kings for my sake, for a testimony to them and to the nations.

19 But when they deliver you up, don't be anxious how or what you will say, for it will be given you in that hour what you will say.

20 For it is not you who speak, but the Spirit of your Father who speaks in you."

23 "But when they persecute you in this city, flee into the next, for most certainly I tell you, you will not have gone through the cities of Israel until the Son of Man has come."

26 "Therefore don't be afraid of them, for there is nothing covered that will not be revealed, or hidden that will not be known.

27 What I tell you in the darkness, speak in the light; and what you hear whispered in the ear, proclaim on the housetops.

28 Don't be afraid of those who kill the body, but are not able to kill the soul. Rather, fear him who is able to destroy both soul and body in Gehenna."

29 "Aren't two sparrows sold for an assarion coin? Not one of them falls to the ground apart from your Father's will.

30 But the very hairs of your head are all numbered.

31 Therefore don't be afraid. You are of more value than many sparrows."

34 "Don't think that I came to send peace on the earth. I didn't come to send peace, but a sword."

NOTE: Being a disciple is not easy, and they face trials and tribulations. They must learn who they can trust. They might have to flee to another city when under duress, but they must always be faithful to God. An assarion coin is a small copper coin. Gehenna was a garbage

pile outside Jerusalem and represented a place of misery.

MATTHEW CHAPTER 11

JESUS GIVES REST

15 "He who has ears to hear, let him hear."

28 "Come to me, all you who labor and are heavily burdened, and I will give you rest.

29 Take my yoke upon you and learn from me, for I am gentle and humble in heart; and you will find rest for your souls.

30 For my yoke is easy, and my burden is light."

NOTE: A yoke is a wooden bar or frame by which two draft animals (such as oxen) are joined at the heads or necks to work together. It can also be a frame fitted to a person's shoulders to carry a load in two equal portions.

MATTHEW CHAPTER 12

A TREE IDENTIFIES THE FRUIT

33 "Either make the tree good and its fruit good, or make the tree corrupt and its fruit corrupt; for the tree is known by its fruit."

NOTE: If you choose to be the person God wants you to be, you produce good fruit; if you rebel against God, you produce bad fruit. Good fruit is love, joy, peace, kindness, goodness, faithfulness, gentleness, self-control, and forbearance. Bad fruit is sinful and evil.

MATTHEW CHAPTER 13

PLANT SEEDS

9 "He who has ears to hear, let him hear."

18 "Hear, then, the parable of the farmer."

43 "Then the righteous will shine like the sun in the Kingdom of their Father. He who has ears to hear, let him hear."

MATTHEW CHAPTER 15

HONOR YOUR MOTHER AND FATHER

4 "For God commanded, 'Honor your father and your mother,' and, 'He who speaks evil of father or mother, let him be put to death.'"

10 He summoned the multitude, and said to them, "Hear, and understand.

11 That which enters into the mouth doesn't defile the man; but that which proceeds out of the mouth, this defiles the man."

14 "Leave them alone. They are blind guides of the blind. If the blind guide the blind, both will fall into a pit."

NOTE: Regarding the mouth, it is not what you eat that defiles you, it what you

think and say. Examples of what can defile a person include what is in a person's heart: evil thoughts, murder, adultery, greed, lust and sexual immorality, slander, envy, pride, wickedness, theft, deceit, and foolishness.

MATTHEW CHAPTER 16

TAKE UP YOUR CROSS AND FOLLOW JESUS

6 Jesus said to them, "Take heed and beware of the yeast of the Pharisees and Sadducees."

24 Then Jesus said to his disciples, "If anyone desires to come after me, let him deny himself, take up his cross, and follow me."

NOTE: The yeast of the Pharisees refers to self-righteous and hypocritical religious leaders who created and promoted overbearing laws.

THE COMMANDS OF MARK

MARK

MARK CHAPTER 1

REPENT OF YOUR SINS

15 ...and saying, "The time is fulfilled, and God's Kingdom is at hand! Repent, and believe in the Good News."

FOLLOW JESUS

17 Jesus said to them, "Come after me, and I will make you into fishers for men."

NOTE: When you follow Jesus, a believer's responsibility is to share the good news of Christianity with other people.

MARK CHAPTER 4

PLANT SEEDS

3 "Listen! Behold, the farmer went out to sow…"

9 He said, "Whoever has ears to hear, let him hear."

23 "If any man has ears to hear, let him hear."

NOTE: The Bible often used stories called parables to help explain a situation better. In this situation, a farmer plants seeds to grow crops. In the same way, a Christian is to "plant" the good news of Christianity and Jesus Christ in other people so they can make Jesus their Lord.

MARK CHAPTER 6

DISCIPLESHIP

7 He called to himself the twelve, and began to send them out two by two; and he gave them authority over the unclean spirits.

8 He commanded them that they should take nothing for their journey, except a staff only: no bread, no wallet, no money in their purse,

9 but to wear sandals, and not put on two tunics.

10 He said to them, "Wherever you enter into a house, stay there until you depart from there.

11 Whoever will not receive you nor hear you, as you depart from there, shake off the dust that is under your feet for a testimony against them. Assuredly, I tell you, it will be more tolerable for Sodom and Gomorrah in the day of judgment than for that city!"

NOTE: Dusting off of the feet is symbolic for those who reject the message of Jesus. Sodom and Gomorrah were destroyed for their wickedness.

MARK CHAPTER 7

LISTEN TO JESUS

14 He called all the multitude to himself, and said to them, "Hear me, all of you, and understand."

16 "If anyone has ears to hear, let him hear!"

MARK CHAPTER 8

TAKE UP YOUR CROSS AND FOLLOW JESUS

15 He warned them, saying, "Take heed: beware of the yeast of the Pharisees and the yeast of Herod."

NOTE: The yeast of Herod refers to his love of political position and power and his malice for other people.

34 He called the multitude to himself with his disciples, and said to them, "Whoever wants to come after me, let him deny himself, and take up his cross, and follow me."

NOTE: Jesus wants us to follow him instead of our own desires. Carrying the cross was the ultimate submission. In those days submission to Rome and carrying a cross meant an execution. But to Jesus, it meant to deny personal desires and follow him.

MARK CHAPTER 9

BE A SERVANT TO EVERYONE

35 He sat down, and called the twelve; and he said to them, "If any man wants to be first, he shall be last of all, and servant of all."

38 John said to him, "Teacher, we saw someone who doesn't follow us casting out demons in your name; and we forbade him, because he doesn't follow us."

39 But Jesus said, "Don't forbid him, for there is no one who will do a mighty work in my name, and be able quickly to speak evil of me."

NOTE: To be first with God, we must be last, in other words, we must be servants to all.

DON'T TOLERATE SIN IN YOURSELF

43-44 "If your hand causes you to stumble, cut it off. It is better for you to enter into life maimed, rather than having your two hands to go into Gehenna, into the unquenchable fire,

45-46 If your foot causes you to stumble, cut it off. It is better for you to enter into life lame, rather than having your two feet to be cast into Gehenna, into the fire that will never be quenched— 'where their worm doesn't die, and the fire is not quenched.'

47 If your eye causes you to stumble, cast it out. It is better for you to enter into God's Kingdom with one eye, rather than having two eyes to be cast into the Gehenna of fire,

48 'where their worm doesn't die, and the fire is not quenched.'

50 Salt is good, but if the salt has lost its saltiness, with what will you season it? Have salt in yourselves, and be at peace with one another."

NOTE: Gehenna is a place of misery once used for human sacrifice and later a smoldering garbage dump. The point being made is not about cutting off body parts but cutting sin out of a person's life.

MARK CHAPTER 10

BE LIKE CHILDREN

9 "What therefore God has joined together, let no man separate."

14 But when Jesus saw it, he was moved with indignation, and said to them, "Allow the little children to come to me! Don't forbid them, for God's Kingdom belongs to such as these."

REMEMBER THE TEN COMMANDMENTS

19 "You know the commandments: 'Do not murder,' 'Do not commit adultery,' 'Do not steal,' 'Do not give false testimony,' 'Do not defraud,' 'Honor your father and mother.'"

SELL YOUR POSSESSIONS, GIVE TO THE POOR, AND FOLLOW JESUS

21 Jesus looking at him loved him, and said to him, "One thing you lack. Go, sell whatever you have, and give to the poor, and you will have treasure in heaven; and come, follow me, taking up the cross."

MARK CHAPTER 11

BELIEVE AND RECEIVE

22 Jesus answered them, "Have faith in God.

23 For most certainly I tell you, whoever may tell this mountain, 'Be taken up and cast into the sea,' and doesn't doubt in his heart, but believes that what he says is happening; he shall have whatever he says.

24 Therefore I tell you, all things whatever you pray and ask for, believe that you have received them, and you shall have them."

NOTE: We should pray with faith, knowing God can do the impossible.

FORGIVE

25 "Whenever you stand praying, forgive, if you have anything against anyone; so that your Father, who is in heaven, may also forgive you your transgressions.

26 But if you do not forgive, neither will your Father in heaven forgive your transgressions."

MARK CHAPTER 12

GIVE TO GOD AND GIVE TO THE GOVERNMENT

17 Jesus answered them, "Render to Caesar the things that are Caesar's, and to God the things that are God's." They marveled greatly at him.

NOTE: Give to the government to support society, but give to God to advance Christianity.

LOVE GOD WITH ALL YOUR HEART

29 Jesus answered, "The greatest is, 'Hear, Israel, the Lord our God, the Lord is one:

30 you shall love the Lord your God with all your heart, and with all your soul, and with all your mind, and with all your strength.' This is the first commandment.

LOVE OTHERS

31 The second is like this, 'You shall love your neighbor as yourself.' There is no other commandment greater than these."

BEWARE OF SCRIBES

38 In his teaching he said to them, "Beware of the scribes, who like to walk in long robes, and to get greetings in the marketplaces,

39 and the best seats in the synagogues, and the best places at feasts:

40 those who devour widows' houses, and for a pretense make long prayers. These will receive greater condemnation."

NOTE: The scribes are religious leaders who exploit people for status, recognition, and respect.

MARK CHAPTER 13

DON'T BE MISLED BY FALSE TEACHERS

5 Jesus, answering, began to tell them, "Be careful that no one leads you astray.

6 For many will come in my name, saying, 'I am he!' and will lead many astray."

ENDURE ALL TRIALS AND BE SAVED

7 "When you hear of wars and rumors of wars, don't be troubled. For those must happen, but the end is not yet.

8 For nation will rise against nation, and kingdom against kingdom. There will be earthquakes in various places. There will be famines and troubles. These things are the beginning of birth pains.

9 But watch yourselves, for they will deliver you up to councils. You will be beaten in synagogues. You will stand before rulers and kings for my sake, for a testimony to them.

10 The Good News must first be preached to all the nations.

11 When they lead you away and deliver you up, don't be anxious beforehand, or premeditate what you will say, but say whatever will be given you in that hour. For it is not you who speak, but the Holy Spirit."

12 "Brother will deliver up brother to death, and the Father his child. Children will rise up against parents, and cause them to be put to death.

13 "You will be hated by all men for my name's sake, but he who endures to the end will be saved.

14 But when you see the abomination of desolation, spoken of by Daniel the prophet, standing where it ought not" (let the reader understand), "then let those who are in Judea flee to the mountains…

15 …and let him who is on the housetop not go down, nor enter in, to take anything out of his house.

16 Let him who is in the field not return back to take his cloak.

17 But woe to those who are with child and to those who nurse babies in those days!

18 Pray that your flight won't be in the winter.

19 For in those days there will be oppression, such as there has not been the like from the beginning of the creation which God created until now, and never will be.

20 Unless the Lord had shortened the days, no flesh would have been saved; but for the sake of the chosen ones, whom he picked out, he shortened the days.

21 Then if anyone tells you, 'Look, here is the Christ!' or, 'Look, there!' don't believe it.

22 For there will arise false christs and false prophets, and will show signs and wonders, that they may lead astray, if possible, even the chosen ones."

23 But you watch. "Behold, I have told you all things beforehand."

28 "Now from the fig tree, learn this parable. When the branch has now become tender, and produces its leaves, you know that the summer is near;

29 even so you also, when you see these things coming to pass, know that it is near, at the doors."

NOTE: Verses 7-29 refer to the signs of the end times.

NO ONE KNOWS WHEN JESUS WILL RETURN

32 "But of that day or that hour no one knows, not even the angels in heaven, nor the Son, but only the Father.

33 Watch, keep alert, and pray; for you don't know when the time is.

KEEP WATCH

35 Watch therefore, for you don't know when the lord of the house is coming, whether at evening, or at midnight, or when the rooster crows, or in the morning;

36 lest coming suddenly he might find you sleeping.

37 What I tell you, I tell all: Watch."

MARK CHAPTER 14

REMEMBER THE BODY AND BLOOD OF JESUS

22 As they were eating, Jesus took bread, and when he had blessed, he broke it, and gave to them, and said, "Take, eat. This is my body."

23 He took the cup, and when he had given thanks, he gave to them. They all drank of it.

24 He said to them, "This is my blood of the new covenant, which is poured out for many."

38 "Watch and pray, that you may not enter into temptation. The spirit indeed is willing, but the flesh is weak."

NOTE: Communion is a time to remember the sacrifice Jesus made on the cross for us, his human death, and his promise to return.

MARK CHAPTER 16

GO INTO THE WORLD AND PREACH THE GOSPEL

15 He said to them, "Go into all the world, and preach the Good News to the whole creation.

16 He who believes and is baptized will be saved; but he who disbelieves will be condemned."

THE COMMANDS
OF LUKE

LUKE

LUKE CHAPTER 3

PROVE THAT YOU HAVE REPENTED

8 "Therefore produce fruits worthy of repentance, and don't begin to say among yourselves, 'We have Abraham for our father;' for I tell you that God is able to raise up children to Abraham from these stones!"

NOTE: Religious connections or lineage does not help a person. Instead, a Christian needs to focus on faith and the fruits of the spirit: Love, compassion, peace, kindness, goodness, gentleness, self-control, faithfulness, and forbearance.

GIVE TO THE POOR

11 He answered them, "He who has two coats, let him give to him who has none. He who has food, let him do likewise."

13 He said to them, "Collect no more than that which is appointed to you."

NOTE: Verse 13 refers to not over-taxing the people.

DON'T EXTORT MONEY

14 Soldiers also asked him, saying, "What about us? What must we do?" He said to them, "Extort from no one by violence, neither accuse anyone wrongfully. Be content with your wages."

LUKE CHAPTER 4

SERVE GOD

4 Jesus answered him, saying, "It is written, 'Man shall not live by bread alone, but by every word of God.'"

8 Jesus answered him, "Get behind me Satan! For it is written, 'You shall worship the Lord your God, and you shall serve him only.'"

12 Jesus answering, said to him, "It has been said, 'You shall not tempt the Lord your God.'"

NOTE: Jesus sets an example for Christians by not giving into temptation and understanding that life is more than physical needs.

LUKE CHAPTER 5

FISH FOR MEN'S SOULS

10 ...and so also were James and John, sons of Zebedee, who were partners with Simon. Jesus said to Simon, "Don't be afraid. From now on you will be catching people alive."

27 After these things he went out, and saw a tax collector named Levi sitting at the tax office, and said to him, "Follow me!"

NOTE: Christians must share their faith and bring people to Jesus Christ.

LUKE CHAPTER 6

LOVE YOUR ENEMIES

22 "Blessed are you when men hate you, and when they exclude and mock you, and throw out your name as evil, for the Son of Man's sake.

23 Rejoice in that day, and leap for joy, for behold, your reward is great in heaven, for their fathers did the same thing to the prophets."

27 "But I tell you who hear: love your enemies, do good to those who hate you,

28 bless those who curse you, and pray for those who mistreat you.

29 To him who strikes you on the cheek, offer also the other; and from him who takes away your cloak, don't withhold your coat also.

30 Give to everyone who asks you, and don't ask him who takes away your goods to give them back again."

31 "As you would like people to do to you, do exactly so to them."

35 "But love your enemies, and do good, and lend, expecting nothing back; and your reward will be great, and you will be children of the Most High; for he is kind toward the unthankful and evil."

36 "Therefore be merciful, even as your Father is also merciful."

37 "Don't judge, and you won't be judged. Don't condemn, and you won't be condemned. Set free, and you will be set free."

38 "Give, and it will be given to you: good measure, pressed down, shaken together, and running over, will be given to you. For with the same measure you measure it will be measured back to you."

NOTE: Most people can love people who love them. The true test is loving our enemies, which is God's plan.

DON'T BE A HYPOCRITE

42 "Or how can you tell your brother, 'Brother, let me remove the speck of chaff that is in your eye,' when you yourself don't see the beam that is in your own eye? You hypocrite! First remove the beam from your own eye, and then you can see clearly to remove the speck of chaff that is in your brother's eye."

LUKE CHAPTER 8

PLANT SEEDS

8 "Other fell into the good ground, and grew, and produced one hundred times as much fruit." As he said these things, he called out, "He who has ears to hear, let him hear!"

18 "Sharing the word of God with others is like a farmer planting seeds in the field. Some seeds will take and grow, and some will not, but like planting a seed, it is essential to share your faith so it can grow in others."

NOTE: Sharing the word of God with others is like a farmer planting seeds in the field. Some seeds will take and grow, and some will not, but like planting a seed, it is essential to share your faith so it can grow in others.

LUKE CHAPTER 9

DISCIPLESHIP TRAVEL

3 He said to them, "Take nothing for your journey—no staffs, nor wallet, nor bread, nor money. Don't have two coats each.

4 Into whatever house you enter, stay there, and depart from there.

5 As many as don't receive you, when you depart from that city, shake off even the dust from your feet for a testimony against them."

NOTE: Dusting off of the feet is symbolic for those who reject the message of Jesus. Sodom and Gomorrah were destroyed for their wickedness.

FOLLOW JESUS

23 He said to all, "If anyone desires to come after me, let him deny himself, take up his cross, and follow me.

50 Jesus said to him, "Don't forbid him, for he who is not against us is for us."

59 He said to another, "Follow me!" But he said, "Lord, allow me first to go and bury my father."

60 But Jesus said to him, "Leave the dead to bury their own dead, but you go and announce God's Kingdom."

NOTE: Jesus wants people to deny their desires and to share the good news and ministry of Jesus Christ.

LUKE CHAPTER 10

THE HARVEST IS GREAT

2 Then he said to them, "The harvest is indeed plentiful, but the laborers are few. Pray therefore to the Lord of the harvest, that he may send out laborers into his harvest.

3 Go your ways. Behold, I send you out as lambs among wolves.

4 Carry no purse, nor wallet, nor sandals. Greet no one on the way.

5 Into whatever house you enter, first say, 'Peace be to this house.'

6 If a son of peace is there, your peace will rest on him; but if not, it will return to you.

7 Remain in that same house, eating and drinking the things they give, for the laborer is worthy of his wages. Don't go from house to house.

8 Into whatever city you enter, and they receive you, eat the things that are set before you

9 Heal the sick who are there, and tell them, 'God's Kingdom has come near to you.'

10 But into whatever city you enter, and they don't receive you, go out into its streets and say,

11 'Even the dust from your city that clings to us, we wipe off against you. Nevertheless know this, that God's Kingdom has come near to you.'

12 I tell you, it will be more tolerable in that day for Sodom than for that city."

NOTE: Again, dusting off of the feet is symbolic for those who reject the message of Jesus. Sodom and Gomorrah were destroyed for their wickedness.

LOVE YOUR GOD WITH ALL YOUR HEART

20 "Nevertheless, don't rejoice in this, that the spirits are subject to you, but rejoice that your names are written in heaven."

27 He answered, "You shall love the Lord your God with all your heart, with all your soul, with all your strength, and with all your mind; and your neighbor as yourself."

28 He said to him, "You have answered correctly. Do this, and you will live."

SHOW MERCY

37 He said, "He who showed mercy on him." Then Jesus said to him, "Go and do likewise."

LUKE CHAPTER 11

HOW YOU SHOULD PRAY

2 He said to them, "When you pray, say, 'Our Father in heaven, may your name be kept holy. May your Kingdom come. May your will be done on earth, as it is in heaven.

3 Give us day by day our daily bread.

4 Forgive us our sins, for we ourselves also forgive everyone who is indebted to us. Bring us not into temptation, but deliver us from the evil one.'"

KEEP SEEKING

9 "I tell you, keep asking, and it will be given you. Keep seeking, and you will find. Keep knocking, and it will be opened to you."

35 "Therefore see whether the light that is in you isn't darkness."

GIVE TO THE POOR

41 "But give for gifts to the needy those things which are within, and behold, all things will be clean to you."

LUKE CHAPTER 12

BEWARE OF PHARISEES

1 Meanwhile, when a multitude of many thousands had gathered together, so much so that they trampled on each other, he began to tell his disciples first of all, "Beware of the yeast of the Pharisees, which is hypocrisy."

NOTE: The yeast of the Pharisees refers to their hypocrisy, love of political position and power, and malice toward other people.

DON'T BE AFRAID

4 "I tell you, my friends, don't be afraid of those who kill the body, and after that have no more that they can do.

5 But I will warn you whom you should fear. Fear him who after he has killed, has power to cast into Gehenna. Yes, I tell you, fear him."

7 "But the very hairs of your head are all counted. Therefore don't be afraid. You are of more value than many sparrows."

11 "When they bring you before the synagogues, the rulers, and the authorities, don't be anxious how or what you will answer, or what you will say;

12 for the Holy Spirit will teach you in that same hour what you must say."

NOTE: Don't be afraid of humans who can kill you, but God, who can throw you into an eternal place of misery.

GUARD AGAINST GREED

15 He said to them, "Beware! Keep yourselves from covetousness, for a man's life doesn't consist of the abundance of the things which he possesses."

DON'T WORRY ABOUT FOOD AND CLOTHES

22 He said to his disciples, "Therefore I tell you, don't be anxious for your life, what you will eat, nor yet for your body, what you will wear."

24 "Consider the ravens: they don't sow, they don't reap, they have no warehouse or barn, and God feeds them. How much more valuable are you than birds!"

27 "Consider the lilies, how they grow. They don't toil, neither do they spin; yet I tell you, even Solomon in all his glory was not arrayed like one of these."

29 "Don't seek what you will eat or what you will drink; neither be anxious."

31 "But seek God's Kingdom, and all these things will be added to you.

32 Don't be afraid, little flock, for it is your Father's good pleasure to give you the Kingdom."

NOTE: Seek God's Kingdom; he will provide for your physical needs.

SELL YOUR POSSESSIONS

33 "Sell that which you have, and give gifts to those in need. Make for yourselves purses which don't grow old, a treasure in the heavens that doesn't fail, where no thief approaches, neither moth destroys."

WAIT FOR HIS RETURN

35 "Let your waist be dressed and your lamps burning.

36 Be like men watching for their lord, when he returns from the wedding feast; that when he comes and knocks, they may immediately open to him.

40 Therefore be ready also, for the Son of Man is coming in an hour that you don't expect him."

SETTLE YOUR DIFFERENCES BEFORE GOING TO COURT

58 "For when you are going with your adversary before the magistrate, try diligently on the way to be released from him, lest perhaps he drag you to the judge, and the judge deliver you to the officer, and the officer throw you into prison."

NOTE: Try to settle your differences before going to court.

LUKE CHAPTER 13

WORK HARD TO ENTER GOD'S KINGDOM

24 "Strive to enter in by the narrow door, for many, I tell you, will seek to enter in and will not be able."

NOTE: Faith and obedience are both critical to God.

LUKE CHAPTER 14

BE HUMBLE, INVITE THE POOR

8 "When you are invited by anyone to a wedding feast, don't sit in the best seat, since perhaps someone more honorable than you might be invited by him,

9 and he who invited both of you would come and tell you, 'Make room for this person.' Then you would begin, with shame, to take the lowest place.

10 But when you are invited, go and sit in the lowest place, so that when he who invited you comes, he may tell you, 'Friend, move up higher.' Then you will be honored in the presence of all who sit at the table with you."

12 He also said to the one who had invited him, "When you make a dinner or a supper, don't call your friends, nor your brothers, nor your kinsmen, nor rich neighbors, or perhaps they might also return the favor, and pay you back.

13 But when you make a feast, ask the poor, the maimed, the lame, or the blind;

14 and you will be blessed, because they don't have the resources to repay you. For you will be repaid in the resurrection of the righteous."

33 "So therefore whoever of you who doesn't renounce all that he has, he can't be my disciple.

34 Salt is good, but if the salt becomes flat and tasteless, with what do you season it?

35 It is fit neither for the soil nor for the manure pile. It is thrown out. He who has ears to hear, let him hear."

NOTE: Be humble, and let others honor you. Additionally, honor the poor and lame.

LUKE CHAPTER 16

USE WORLDLY RESOURCES TO BENEFIT OTHERS

9 "I tell you, make for yourselves friends by means of unrighteous mammon, so that when you fail, they may receive you into the eternal tents."

NOTE: When greed and striving for material possessions fail, turn to God and focus on heaven.

LUKE CHAPTER 17

REBUKE SIN

3 "Be careful. If your brother sins against you, rebuke him. If he repents, forgive him.

4 If he sins against you seven times in the day, and seven times returns, saying, 'I repent,' you shall forgive him."

FOLLOW JESUS, DON'T LOOK BACK

10 "Even so you also, when you have done all the things that are commanded you, say, 'We are unworthy servants. We have done our duty.'"

32 "Remember Lot's wife!

33 Whoever seeks to save his life loses it, but whoever loses his life preserves it."

NOTE: Some people will love their life, relationships, wealth, and pleasure, but God wants you to follow him.

LUKE CHAPTER 18

KEEP ASKING

6 The Lord said, "Listen to what the unrighteous judge says."

NOTE: A widow wore down a judge by her constant requests, and likewise, God wants his people to seek him continually.

BE LIKE CHILDREN

16 Jesus summoned them, saying, "Allow the little children to come to me, and don't hinder them, for God's Kingdom belongs to such as these.

REMEMBER THE COMMANDMENTS

20 You know the commandments: 'Don't commit adultery,' 'Don't murder,' 'Don't steal,' 'Don't give false testimony,' 'Honor your father and your mother.'"

NOTE: The question from Verse 18 is related to Verse 20. 'Good Teacher, what should I do to inherit eternal life?'

LUKE CHAPTER 20

GIVE TO CAESAR, GIVE TO GOD

25 He said to them, "Then give to Caesar the things that are Caesar's, and to God the things that are God's."

NOTE: Caesar represents paying taxes to the government and giving to and supporting the church.

BEWARE OF TEACHERS OF THE LAW

46 "Beware of those scribes who like to walk in long robes, and love greetings in the marketplaces, the best seats in the synagogues, and the best places at feasts…"

NOTE: Scribes wanted to be known for who they were, rather than what they were teaching.

LUKE CHAPTER 21

KEEP WATCH FOR THE RETURN OF JESUS

8 He said, "Watch out that you don't get led astray, for many will come in my name, saying, 'I am he,' and, 'The time is at hand.' Therefore don't follow them.

9 When you hear of wars and disturbances, don't be terrified, for these things must happen first, but the end won't come immediately."

GOD WILL ANSWER THROUGH YOU

12 (Background for Verse 14) "But before all these things, they will lay their hands on you and will persecute you, delivering you up to synagogues and prisons, bringing you before kings and governors for my name's sake.

14 Settle it therefore in your hearts not to meditate beforehand how to answer,

15 for I will give you a mouth and wisdom which all your adversaries will not be able to withstand or to contradict."

19 "By your endurance you will win your lives."

NOTE: During times of trouble, God will give you the right words to say, and by your endurance, you will win your eternal souls.

THE KINGDOM OF GOD IS NEAR

21 "Then let those who are in Judea flee to the mountains. Let those who are in the middle of her depart. Let those who are in the country not enter therein."

28 "But when these things begin to happen, look up and lift up your heads, because your redemption is near."

29 He told them a parable. "See the fig tree and all the trees.

30 When they are already budding, you see it and know by your own selves that the summer is already near.

31 Even so you also, when you see these things happening, know that God's Kingdom is near."

34 "So be careful, or your hearts will be loaded down with carousing, drunkenness, and cares of this life, and that day will come on you suddenly."

36 "Therefore be watchful all the time, praying that you may be counted worthy to escape all these things that will happen, and to stand before the Son of Man."

NOTE: Do not waste time with the pleasures of an earthly life. Instead, live a life that will help you escape eternal suffering and be considered a faithful servant on judgment day.

LUKE CHAPTER 22

REMEMBER HIS BODY AND BLOOD

17 He received a cup, and when he had given thanks, he said, "Take this, and share it among yourselves…"

19 He took bread, and when he had given thanks, he broke, and gave it to them, saying, "This is my body which is given for you. Do this in memory of me."

NOTE: Remember that communion is a way to honor the sacrifice of Jesus, who shed his blood and died on the cross for our sins.

THE GREATEST ARE SERVANTS

25 He said to them, "The kings of the nations lord it over them, and those who have authority over them are called 'benefactors.'

26 But not so with you. But one who is the greater among you, let him become as the younger, and one who is governing, as one who serves."

36 Then he said to them, "But now, whoever has a purse, let him take it, and likewise a wallet. Whoever has none, let him sell his cloak, and buy a sword."

40 When he was at the place, he said to them, "Pray that you don't enter into temptation."

46 and said to them, "Why do you sleep? Rise and pray that you may not enter into temptation."

NOTE: This section refers to servants who need to be alert and avoid the temptations around them.

THE COMMANDS OF JOHN

JOHN

JOHN CHAPTER 1

FOLLOW JESUS

43 On the next day, he was determined to go out into Galilee, and he found Philip. Jesus said to him, "Follow me."

JOHN CHAPTER 2

THE FATHER'S HOUSE IS NOT A MARKETPLACE

7 Jesus said to them, "Fill the water pots with water." So they filled them up to the brim.

16 To those who sold the doves, he said, "Take these things out of here! Don't make my Father's house a marketplace!"

NOTE: The temple grounds were to be used to pray, praise, and find God, not as a market for profit.

JOHN CHAPTER 3

YOU MUST BE BORN AGAIN

7 "Don't marvel that I said to you, 'You must be born anew.'"

NOTE: Being born again is done through the Holy Spirit from God within a person.

JOHN CHAPTER 4

HUMAN SOULS ARE READY FOR HARVESTING

35 "Don't you say, 'There are yet four months until the harvest?' Behold, I tell you, lift up your eyes and look at the fields, that they are white for harvest already."

NOTE: This is a parable in which the white tips of wheat are ready for harvesting. By the same token, people are prepared to be harvested by sharing the good news of Jesus Christ.

JOHN CHAPTER 5

STOP SINNING

14 Afterward Jesus found him in the temple, and said to him, "Behold, you are made well. Sin no more, so that nothing worse happens to you."

39 "You search the Scriptures, because you think that in them you have eternal life; and these are they which testify about me."

NOTE: Remember, all the scriptures point to Jesus being the way.

JOHN CHAPTER 6

SEEK ETERNAL LIFE, NOT FOOD

27 "Don't work for the food which perishes, but for the food which remains to eternal life, which the Son of Man will give to you. For God the Father has sealed him."

43 Therefore Jesus answered them, "Don't murmur among yourselves."

NOTE: To murmur is to complain or grumble.

JOHN CHAPTER 7

WORKING ON THE SABBATH

23 "If a boy receives circumcision on the Sabbath, that the law of Moses may not be broken, are you angry with me, because I made a man completely healthy on the Sabbath?

24 Don't judge according to appearance, but judge righteous judgment."

Note: The question in Verse 23 leads to Verse 24. Jesus wants people to understand the importance of actual healing rather than the fact that it happened on the Sabbath.

JOHN CHAPTER 12

TRUST IN THE LIGHT

35 Jesus therefore said to them, "Yet a little while the light is with you. Walk while you have the light, that darkness doesn't overtake you. He who walks in the darkness doesn't know where he is going.

36 While you have the light, believe in the light, that you may become children of light." Jesus said these things, and he departed and hid himself from them.

NOTE: The light symbolizes God's message, shown by walking with Jesus and his testimony, which is the right way.

JOHN CHAPTER 13

WASH EACH OTHER'S FEET

14 "If I then, the Lord and the Teacher, have washed your feet, you also ought to wash one another's feet."

15 "For I have given you an example, that you should also do as I have done to you."

34 "A new commandment I give to you, that you love one another. Just as I have loved you, you also love one another."

NOTE: Regardless of one's position in life, being a servant is an expression of respect and love.

JOHN CHAPTER 14

TRUST IN GOD, TRUST IN JESUS

1 "Don't let your heart be troubled. Believe in God. Believe also in me."

11 "Believe me that I am in the Father, and the Father in me; or else believe me for the very works' sake."

13 "Whatever you will ask in my name, I will do it, that the Father may be glorified in the Son."

15 "If you love me, keep my commandments."

27 "Peace I leave with you. My peace I give to you; not as the world gives, I give to you. Don't let your heart be troubled, neither let it be fearful."

NOTE: Verse 15 is essential and the reason for this book. We are saved by faith that Jesus died on the cross for us, but this does not mean we can behave anyway in any manner we choose. Jesus connects a person's love to him according to their obedience to his teachings and related scripture.

JOHN CHAPTER 15

LIVE IN JESUS, LOVE EACH OTHER

4 "Remain in me, and I in you. As the branch can't bear fruit by itself unless it remains in the vine, so neither can you, unless you remain in me."

9 "Even as the Father has loved me, I also have loved you. Remain in my love."

12 "This is my commandment, that you love one another, even as I have loved you."

17 "I command these things to you, that you may love one another."

NOTE: Jesus wants people to stay close to him, his words, his teachings, and his example so that they can produce fruit for the Kingdom of God.

JOHN CHAPTER 16

ASK, AND YOU WILL RECEIVE

24 "Until now, you have asked nothing in my name. Ask, and you will receive, that your joy may be made full."

33 "I have told you these things, that in me you may have peace. In the world you have trouble; but cheer up! I have overcome the world."

NOTE: An earthly existence will bring trials and tribulation, but cheer up—Jesus has overcome the world by his death on the cross.

JOHN CHAPTER 20

BE A DISCIPLE

21 Jesus therefore said to them again, "Peace be to you. As the Father has sent me, even so I send you."

RECEIVE THE HOLY SPIRIT

22 When he had said this, he breathed on them, and said to them, "Receive the Holy Spirit!

23 If you forgive anyone's sins, they have been forgiven them. If you retain anyone's sins, they have been retained."

NOTE: Remember, Jesus and God are the ultimate deciders regarding who can be forgiven, but he guides his followers to discern the truth.

JOHN CHAPTER 21

FEED HIS SHEEP

15 So when they had eaten their breakfast, Jesus said to Simon Peter, "Simon, son of Jonah, do you love me more than these?" He said to him, "Yes, Lord; you know that I have affection for you."

16 He said to him again a second time, "Simon, son of Jonah, do you love me?" He said to him, "Yes, Lord; you know that I have affection for you." He said to him, "Tend my sheep."

17 He said to him the third time, "Simon, son of Jonah, do you have affection for me?" Peter was grieved because he asked him the third time, "Do you have affection for me?" He said to him,

"Lord, you know everything. You know that I have affection for you." Jesus said to him, "Feed my sheep."

NOTE: Peter had denied Jesus three times, and so Jesus asked Peter three times if Peter even loved him. Jesus challenged him, but Jesus showed that he still loved Peter despite Peter's betrayal and showed Peter that love is vitally important.

AS FOR YOU, FOLLOW JESUS

19 Now he said this, signifying what kind of death he would glorify God. When he had said this, he said to him, "Follow me."

22 Jesus said to him, "If I desire that he stay until I come, what is that to you? You follow me."

NOTE: Regardless of the circumstances, we should always follow Jesus.

THE COMMANDS
OF ACTS

ACTS

ACTS CHAPTER 2

REPENT OF YOUR SINS AND BE BAPTIZED

38 Peter said to them, "Repent, and be baptized, every one of you, in the name of Jesus Christ for the forgiveness of sins, and you will receive the gift of the Holy Spirit."

ACTS CHAPTER 3

REPENT OF YOUR SINS

19 "Repent therefore, and turn again, that your sins may be blotted out, so that there may come times of refreshing from the presence of the Lord…"

NOTE: Repenting doesn't mean to apologize; it means acknowledging that your sins are wrong and God's way is right and stopping sinning. Then, you can refresh yourself with the faith, love, and hope that Jesus and the Holy Spirit provide.

ACTS CHAPTER 8

REPENT OF WICKEDNESS

22 Repent therefore of this, your wickedness, and ask God if perhaps the thought of your heart may be forgiven you.

ACTS CHAPTER 10

IF GOD CALLS IT CLEAN, DON'T CALL IT IMPURE

15 A voice came to him again the second time, "What God has cleansed, you must not call unclean."

NOTE: What makes a person unclean is not the food they put in their body but the sin in a person's heart.

PREACH EVERYWHERE

42 He commanded us to preach to the people and to testify that this is he who is appointed by God as the Judge of the living and the dead.

ACTS CHAPTER 13

DON'T MOCK THE TRUTH

40 Beware therefore, lest that come on you which is spoken in the prophets:

41 'Behold, you scoffers, and wonder, and perish; for I work a work in your days, a work which you will in no way believe, if one declares it to you.'

NOTE: God warns us to accept his message or die, yet the scoffers would not accept a proven event even if they knew about it.

ACTS CHAPTER 15

ABSTAINING

20 "…but that we write to them that they abstain from the pollution of idols, from sexual immorality, from what is strangled, and from blood.

29 that you abstain from things sacrificed to idols, from blood, from things strangled, and from sexual immorality, from which if you keep yourselves, it will be well with you. Farewell."

NOTE: It's crucial to stay away from idolatry and sexual immorality.

ACTS CHAPTER 17

PUT AWAY IDOLS

30 The times of ignorance therefore God overlooked. But now he commands that all people everywhere should repent…

ACTS CHAPTER 20

FEED GOD'S PEOPLE

28 Take heed, therefore, to yourselves, and to all the flock, in which the Holy Spirit has made you overseers, to shepherd the assembly of the Lord and God which he purchased with his own blood.

NOTE: The elders or Pastors, or those leading the flock, need to guide God's people.

BEWARE OF FALSE TEACHERS

29 For I know that after my departure, vicious wolves will enter in among you, not sparing the flock.

30 Men will arise from among your own selves, speaking perverse things, to draw away the disciples after them.

31 Therefore watch, remembering that for a period of three years I didn't cease to admonish everyone night and day with tears.

NOTE: Avoid those people who can lead you astray.

THE COMMANDS
OF ROMANS

ROMANS

ROMANS CHAPTER 6

DON'T SERVE SIN

11 Thus consider yourselves also to be dead to sin, but alive to God in Christ Jesus our Lord.

12 Therefore don't let sin reign in your mortal body, that you should obey it in its lusts.

13 Also, do not present your members to sin as instruments of unrighteousness, but present yourselves to God as alive from the dead, and your members as instruments of righteousness to God.

NOTE: Turning from sin shows you are alive for Jesus and living in righteousness for him.

ROMANS CHAPTER 11

DO NOT BRAG (THE GENTILES BLESSING)

17 But if some of the branches were broken off, and you, being a wild olive, were grafted in among them and became partaker with them of the root and of the richness of the olive tree,

18 don't boast over the branches. But if you boast, it is not you who support the root, but the root supports you.

21 ...for if God didn't spare the natural branches, neither will he spare you.

NOTE: Gentile Christians were grafted into the tree of Christianity when others refused the salvation of Jesus Christ. But he warns the Gentiles to be humble and not brag about this great gift.

ROMANS CHAPTER 12

GIVE YOUR BODIES TO GOD

1 Therefore I urge you, brothers, by the mercies of God, to present your bodies a living sacrifice, holy, acceptable to God, which is your spiritual service.

NOTE: In the Old Testament, animal sacrifices were used under the old covenant sacrificial system. Here, we see God wants his people to use their body as a living sacrifice and run from sin.

BE A NEW PERSON

2 Don't be conformed to this world, but be transformed by the renewing of your mind, so that you may prove what is the good, well-pleasing, and perfect will of God.

NOTE: Mind renewal means avoiding focusing on earthly pleasures, material possessions, and earthly status and focusing on what pleases God.

MEASURE YOURSELF BY FAITH

3 For I say through the grace that was given me, to every man who is among you, not to think of himself more highly than he ought to think; but to think reasonably, as God has apportioned to each person a measure of faith.

USE YOUR GOD-GIVEN GIFTS

6 ...having gifts differing according to the grace that was given to us: if prophecy, let's prophesy according to the proportion of our faith;

7 or service, let's give ourselves to service; or he who teaches, to his teaching;

8 or he who exhorts, to his exhorting; he who gives, let him do it with generosity; he who rules, with diligence; he who shows mercy, with cheerfulness.

NOTE: The gift of exhortation is the Spiritual ability to build someone up by challenging them to do better.

LOVE PEOPLE

9 Let love be without hypocrisy. Abhor that which is evil. Cling to that which is good.

10 In love of the brothers be tenderly affectionate to one another; in honor preferring one another;

NOTE: Preferring one another is to honor and enjoy each other's company.

WORK HARD

11 not lagging in diligence; fervent in spirit; serving the Lord;

BE PATIENT

12 rejoicing in hope; enduring in troubles; continuing steadfastly in prayer;

HELP GOD'S CHILDREN

13 contributing to the needs of the saints; given to hospitality.

BLESS THE PERSECUTORS

14 Bless those who persecute you; bless, and don't curse.

HOW TO TREAT OTHERS

15 Rejoice with those who rejoice. Weep with those who weep.

16 Be of the same mind one toward another. Don't set your mind on high things, but associate with the humble. Don't be wise in your own conceits.

17 Repay no one evil for evil. Respect what is honorable in the sight of all men.

18 If it is possible, as much as it is up to you, be at peace with all men.

19 Don't seek revenge yourselves, beloved, but give place to God's wrath. For it is written, "Vengeance belongs to me; I will repay, says the Lord."

20 Therefore "If your enemy is hungry, feed him. If he is thirsty, give him a drink; for in doing so, you will heap coals of fire on his head."

21 Don't be overcome by evil, but overcome evil with good.

ROMANS CHAPTER 13

OBEY THE AUTHORITIES AND LAWS

1 Let every soul be in subjection to the higher authorities, for there is no authority except from God, and those who exist are ordained by God.

3 For rulers are not a terror to the good work, but to the evil. Do you desire to have no fear of the authority? Do that which is good, and you will have praise from the authority,

4 for he is a servant of God to you for good. But if you do that which is evil, be afraid, for he doesn't bear the sword in vain; for he is a servant of God, an avenger for wrath to him who does evil.

5 Therefore you need to be in subjection, not only because of the wrath, but also for conscience' sake.

6 For this reason you also pay taxes, for they are servants of God's service, continually doing this very thing.

7 Therefore give everyone what you owe: if you owe taxes, pay taxes; if customs, then customs; if respect, then respect; if honor, then honor.

NOTE: God shows us here that all authority is created by God, even on earth, and that we should pay taxes and obey laws. If we do evil, we should be fearful because we will be punished.

LOVE YOUR NEIGHBOR

8 Owe no one anything, except to love one another; for he who loves his neighbor has fulfilled the law.

9 For the commandments, "You shall not commit adultery," "You shall not murder," "You shall not steal," "You shall not covet," and whatever other commandments there are, are all summed up in this saying, namely, "You shall love your neighbor as yourself."

NOTE: The Ten Commandments and obeying God's laws are very important, and much of this instruction is related to loving each other.

PUT ON THE SHINING ARMOR OF RIGHT LIVING

12 The night is far gone, and the day is near. Let's therefore throw off the deeds of darkness, and let's put on the armor of light.

LIVE DECENT LIVES

13 Let's walk properly, as in the day; not in reveling and drunkenness, not in sexual promiscuity and lustful acts, and not in strife and jealousy.

14 But put on the Lord Jesus Christ, and make no provision for the flesh, for its lusts.

ROMANS CHAPTER 14

ACCEPT OTHERS

1 Now accept one who is weak in faith, but not for disputes over opinions.

EATING GUIDELINES

3 Don't let him who eats despise him who doesn't eat. Don't let him who doesn't eat judge him who eats, for God has accepted him.

ACCEPT DIFFERENT CHRISTIAN BELIEFS

5 One man esteems one day as more important. Another esteems every day alike. Let each man be fully assured in his own mind.

6 He who observes the day, observes it to the Lord; and he who does not observe the day, to the Lord he does not observe it. He who eats, eats to the Lord, for he gives God thanks. He who doesn't eat, to the Lord he doesn't eat, and gives God thanks.

7 For none of us lives to himself, and none dies to himself.

13 Therefore let's not judge one another any more, but judge this rather, that no man put a stumbling block in his brother's way, or an occasion for falling.

15 Yet if because of food your brother is grieved, you walk no longer in love. Don't destroy with your food him for whom Christ died.

16 Then don't let your good be slandered…

19 So then, let's follow after things which make for peace, and things by which we may build one another up.

20 Don't overthrow God's work for food's sake. All things indeed are clean, however it is evil for that man who creates a stumbling block by eating.

22 Do you have faith? Have it to yourself before God. Happy is he who doesn't judge himself in that which he approves.

NOTE: Some people will have differing beliefs within the context of Christianity. Accept them unless what they say contradicts what God puts forth in scripture.

ROMANS CHAPTER 15

HELP OTHERS

1 Now we who are strong ought to bear the weaknesses of the weak, and not to please ourselves.

2 Let each one of us please his neighbor for that which is good, to be building him up.

7 Therefore accept one another, even as Christ also accepted you, to the glory of God.

10 Again he says, "Rejoice, you Gentiles, with his people."

11 Again, "Praise the Lord, all you Gentiles! Let all the peoples praise him."

ROMANS CHAPTER 16

GREET EACH OTHER

16 Greet one another with a holy kiss. The assemblies of Christ greet you.

AVOID DIVISIONS

17 Now I beg you, brothers, look out for those who are causing the divisions and occasions of stumbling, contrary to the doctrine which you learned, and turn away from them.

NOTE: Stay focused on the path Jesus Christ has put you on and don't be distracted by those who can take you off that path.

THE COMMANDS OF I CORINTHIANS

I CORINTHIANS

I CORINTHIANS CHAPTER 1

LIVE IN HARMONY

10 Now I beg you, brothers, through the name of our Lord, Jesus Christ, that you all speak the same thing, and that there be no divisions among you, but that you be perfected together in the same mind and in the same judgment.

NOTE: God wants like-minded people who do not waste time arguing so they can share the good news of Jesus Christ with others.

I CORINTHIANS CHAPTER 3

UNDERSTAND TRUE WISDOM (BECOME A FOOL)

18 Let no one deceive himself. If anyone thinks that he is wise among you in this world, let him become a fool, that he may become wise.

NOTE: Human wisdom cannot compare to God's wisdom.

DON'T BOAST

21 Therefore let no one boast in men. For all things are yours,

NOTE: Don't boast of men, but what God has done.

I CORINTHIANS CHAPTER 4

DON'T JUDGE

1 So let a man think of us as Christ's servants, and stewards of God's mysteries.

5 Therefore judge nothing before the time, until the Lord comes, who will both bring to light the hidden things of darkness, and reveal the counsels of the hearts. Then each man will get his praise from God.

NOTE: While confronting Christians is important, God is their ultimate judge.

16 I beg you therefore, be imitators of me.

NOTE: Paul wants Christians to follow his example as a Christian, as Paul followed God's example.

I CORINTHIANS CHAPTER 5

CAST OUT EVIL

4 In the name of our Lord Jesus Christ, you being gathered together, and my spirit, with the power of our Lord Jesus Christ,

5 are to deliver such a one to Satan for the destruction of the flesh, that the spirit may be saved in the day of the Lord Jesus.

NOTE: God does not want sin tolerated in the church, which affects other believers.

7 Purge out the old yeast, that you may be a new lump, even as you are unleavened. For indeed Christ, our Passover, has been sacrificed in our place.

NOTE: Purging yeast is to eliminate sin and renew the church.

WHO TO JUDGE

9 I wrote to you in my letter to have no company with sexual sinners;

10 yet not at all meaning with the sexual sinners of this world, or with the covetous and extortionists, or with idolaters; for then you would have to leave the world.

11 But as it is, I wrote to you not to associate with anyone who is called a brother who is a sexual sinner, or covetous, or an idolater, or a slanderer, or a drunkard, or an extortionist. Don't even eat with such a person.

13 But those who are outside, God judges. "Put away the wicked man from among yourselves."

NOTE: God does not want us to avoid unbelievers but those who claim to be Christians and continue in their wicked ways.

I CORINTHIANS CHAPTER 6

HANDLING LEGAL DISPUTES

4 If then you have to judge things pertaining to this life, do you set them to judge who are of no account in the assembly?

NOTE: Christians should try to handle matters between themselves rather than a secular court.

RUN FROM SIN

9 Or don't you know that the unrighteous will not inherit God's Kingdom? Don't be deceived. Neither the sexually immoral, nor idolaters, nor adulterers, nor male prostitutes, nor homosexuals,

10 nor thieves, nor covetous, nor drunkards, nor slanderers, nor extortionists, will inherit God's Kingdom.

18 Flee sexual immorality! "Every sin that a man does is outside the body," but he who commits sexual immorality sins against his own body.

NOTE: Sex within a marriage is a loving and beautiful act between a husband and his wife. However, sex outside of marriage is to follow selfish and sinful desires that harm the body.

I CORINTHIANS CHAPTER 7

MARRIAGE AND SEX

2 But, because of sexual immoralities, let each man have his own wife, and let each woman have her own husband.

3 Let the husband give his wife the affection owed her, and likewise also the wife her husband.

4 The wife doesn't have authority over her own body, but the husband. Likewise also the husband doesn't have authority over his own body, but the wife.

5 Don't deprive one another, unless it is by consent for a season, that you may give yourselves to fasting and prayer, and may be together again, that Satan doesn't tempt you because of your lack of self-control.

NOTE: Husbands and wives should cater to each other's sexual needs.

10 But to the married I command—not I, but the Lord—that the wife not leave her husband

11 (but if she departs, let her remain unmarried, or else be reconciled to her husband), and that the husband not leave his wife.

15 Yet if the unbeliever departs, let there be separation. The brother or the sister is not under bondage in such cases, but God has called us in peace.

CIRCUMCISION

18 Was anyone called having been circumcised? Let him not become uncircumcised. Has anyone been called in uncircumcision? Let him not be circumcised.

NOTE: Before Christ died, God wanted circumcision for his followers, but once Jesus died on the cross, it was no longer necessary.

DO GOD'S WORK

20 Let each man stay in that calling in which he was called.

SLAVES DON'T WORRY

21 Were you called being a bondservant? Don't let that bother you, but if you get an opportunity to become free, use it.

23 You were bought with a price. Don't become bondservants of men.

NOTE: Bondservants, or slaves here on earth, don't fret; you are a servant to Jesus Christ.

BE FREE FROM PRIDE AND FEAR

24 Brothers, let each man, in whatever condition he was called, stay in that condition with God.

MARRIAGE AND DIVORCE

27 Are you bound to a wife? Don't seek to be freed. Are you free from a wife? Don't seek a wife.

28 But if you marry, you have not sinned. If a virgin marries, she has not sinned. Yet such will have oppression in the flesh, and I want to spare you.

29 But I say this, brothers: the time is short, that from now on, both those who have wives may be as though they had none;

NOTE: Even husbands with wives should focus on and share the good news of Jesus Christ.

AVOID DISTRACTIONS

30 and those who weep, as though they didn't weep; and those who rejoice, as though they didn't rejoice; and those who buy, as though they didn't possess;

31 and those who use the world, as not using it to the fullest. For the mode of this world passes away.

NOTE: Our focus should not be on human desires and possessions but rather on God's work to be done.

UNMARRIED BENEFITS

32 But I desire to have you to be free from cares. He who is unmarried is concerned for the things of the Lord, how he may please the Lord;

33 but he who is married is concerned about the things of the world, how he may please his wife.

34 There is also a difference between a wife and a virgin. The unmarried woman cares about the things of the Lord, that she may be holy both in body and in spirit. But she who is married cares about the things of the world—how she may please her husband.

35 This I say for your own profit; not that I may ensnare you, but for that which is appropriate, and that you may attend to the Lord without distraction.

36 But if any man thinks that he is behaving inappropriately toward his virgin, if she is past the flower of her age, and if need so requires, let him do what he desires. He doesn't sin. Let them marry.

37 But he who stands steadfast in his heart, having no urgency, but has power over his own will, and has determined in his own heart to keep his own virgin, does well.

38 So then both he who gives his own virgin in marriage does well, and he who doesn't give her in marriage does better.

I CORINTHIANS CHAPTER 8

EATING CONSCIENCE

9 But be careful that by no means does this liberty of yours become a stumbling block to the weak.

NOTE: A person is free to eat a certain way, but it may cause another Christian to stumble in their consciousness, so let‹s be sensitive to others with differing but acceptable beliefs.

I CORINTHIANS CHAPTER 9

9 For it is written in the law of Moses, "You shall not muzzle an ox while it treads out the grain." Is it for the oxen that God cares,

NOTE: Those who plow should receive part of the harvest.

RUN TO WIN

24 Don't you know that those who run in a race all run, but one receives the prize? Run like that, that you may win.

NOTE: Like an athlete in training, a Christian must prepare himself for the sacrifice of living a Christian life.

I CORINTHIANS CHAPTER 10

AVOID IDOLATRY

7 Don't be idolaters, as some of them were. As it is written, "The people sat down to eat and drink, and rose up to play."

NOTE: This idolatry in this reference refers to worshipping a golden calf.

AVOID SEXUAL IMMORALITY

8 Let's not commit sexual immorality, as some of them committed, and in one day twenty-three thousand fell.

DON'T TEST GOD

9 Let's not test Christ as some of them tested, and perished by the serpents.

10 Don't grumble, as some of them also grumbled, and perished by the destroyer.

12 Therefore let him who thinks he stands be careful that he doesn't fall.

14 Therefore, my beloved, flee from idolatry.

NOTE: To grumble is to complain.

THINK OF OTHERS

15 I speak as to wise men. Judge what I say.

24 Let no one seek his own, but each one his neighbor's good.

FOOD OFFERED TO IDOLS

25 Whatever is sold in the butcher shop, eat, asking no question for the sake of conscience,

27 But if one of those who don't believe invites you to a meal, and you are inclined to go, eat whatever is set before you, asking no questions for the sake of conscience.

28 But if anyone says to you, "This was offered to idols," don't eat it for the sake of the one who told you, and for the sake of conscience. For "the earth is the Lord's, with all its fullness."

29 Conscience, I say, not your own, but the other's conscience. For why is my liberty judged by another conscience?

DO ALL FOR GOD

31 Whether therefore you eat, or drink, or whatever you do, do all to the glory of God.

32 Give no occasion for stumbling, whether to Jews, or to Greeks, or to the assembly of God;

I CORINTHIANS CHAPTER 11

HEAD COVERINGS

1 Be imitators of me, even as I also am of Christ.

5 But every woman praying or prophesying with her head uncovered dishonors her head. For it is one and the same thing as if she were shaved.

6 For if a woman is not covered, let her hair also be cut off. But if it is shameful for a woman to have her hair cut off or be shaved, let her be covered.

7 For a man indeed ought not to have his head covered, because he is the image and glory of God, but the woman is the glory of the man.

13 Judge for yourselves. Is it appropriate that a woman pray to God unveiled?

NOTE: Women should wear head coverings for public worship, and men should not.

PARTAKE IN MY BODY

24 When he had given thanks, he broke it and said, "Take, eat. This is my body, which is broken for you. Do this in memory of me."

PARTAKE IN MY BLOOD

25 In the same way he also took the cup, after supper, saying, "This cup is the new covenant in my blood. Do this, as often as you drink, in memory of me."

28 But let a man examine himself, and so let him eat of the bread, and drink of the cup.

33 Therefore, my brothers, when you come together to eat, wait for one another.

34 But if anyone is hungry, let him eat at home, lest your coming together be for judgment. The rest I will set in order whenever I come.

NOTE: The Lord's Supper and partaking in the body and blood help us grow spiritually, but they must be done entirely honoring the

body and blood and the ultimate sacrifice of Jesus Christ.

I CORINTHIANS CHAPTER 12

DESIRE GODLY GIFTS

31 But earnestly desire the best gifts. Moreover, I show a most excellent way to you.

I CORINTHIANS CHAPTER 14

MAKE LOVE YOUR HIGHEST GOAL AND ASK FOR SPECIAL ABILITIES

1 Follow after love and earnestly desire spiritual gifts, but especially that you may prophesy.

12 So also you, since you are zealous for spiritual gifts, seek that you may abound to the building up of the assembly.

NOTE: Seek gifts that uplift the whole church.

TONGUES REQUIRE INTERPRETATION

13 Therefore let him who speaks in another language pray that he may interpret.

PLAN NO EVIL

20 Brothers, don't be children in thoughts, yet in malice be babies, but in thoughts be mature.

STRENGTHEN EACH OTHER

26 What is it then, brothers? When you come together, each one of you has a psalm, has a teaching, has a revelation, has another language, or has an interpretation. Let all things be done to build each other up.

NOTE: Each person contributes to building up the church.

SPEAKING IN TONGUES

27 If any man speaks in another language, let it be two, or at the most three, and in turn; and let one interpret.

28 But if there is no interpreter, let him keep silent in the assembly, and let him speak to himself, and to God.

SPEAKING IN PROPHESY

29 Let the prophets speak, two or three, and let the others discern.

30 But if a revelation is made to another sitting by, let the first keep silent.

WOMEN SILENT IN THE CHURCH

34 Let the wives be quiet in the assemblies, for it has not been permitted for them to be talking except in submission, as the law also says,

35 if they desire to learn anything. "Let them ask their own husbands at home, for it is shameful for a wife to be talking in the assembly."

37 If any man thinks himself to be a prophet, or spiritual, let him recognize the things which

I write to you, that they are the commandment of the Lord.

38 But if anyone is ignorant, let him be ignorant.

39 Therefore, brothers, desire earnestly to prophesy, and don't forbid speaking with other languages.

40 Let all things be done decently and in order.

I CORINTHIANS CHAPTER 15

AVOID BAD COMPANY

33 Don't be deceived! "Evil companionships corrupt good morals."

NOTE: Make sure your relationships with unbelievers don't take you away from serving Jesus Christ.

STOP SINNING

34 Wake up righteously, and don't sin, for some have no knowledge of God. I say this to your shame.

WORK ENTHUSIASTICALLY FOR THE LORD

58 Therefore, my beloved brothers, be steadfast, immovable, always abounding in the Lord's work, because you know that your labor is not in vain in the Lord.

I CORINTHIANS CHAPTER 16

MONEY COLLECTION (TITHING)

1 Now concerning the collection for the saints, as I commanded the assemblies of Galatia, you do likewise.

2 On the first day of every week, let each one of you save, as he may prosper, that no collections are made when I come.

NOTE: At this time collections were made to support the Christians in Jerusalem.

STAND FIRM

13 Watch! Stand firm in the faith! Be courageous! Be strong!

SHOW KINDNESS AND LOVE

14 Let all that you do be done in love.

20 All the brothers greet you. Greet one another with a holy kiss.

22 If any man doesn't love the Lord Jesus Christ, let him be cursed. Come, Lord!

THE COMMANDS
OF 2 CORINTHIANS

2 CORINTHIANS

2 CORINTHIANS CHAPTER 6

OPEN YOUR HEART TO SALVATION

1 Working together, we entreat also that you do not receive the grace of God in vain,

NOTE: Don't ignore God's gift of salvation.

2 for he says, "At an acceptable time I listened to you. In a day of salvation I helped you." Behold, now is the acceptable time. Behold, now is the day of salvation.

13 Now in return, I speak as to my children: you also open your hearts.

NOTE: God wants people to have an open heart to God's messengers.

DON'T TEAM WITH WICKEDNESS

14 Don't be unequally yoked with unbelievers, for what fellowship do righteousness and iniquity have? Or what fellowship does light have with darkness?

17 Therefore 'Come out from among them, and be separate,' says the Lord. 'Touch no unclean thing. I will receive you.

NOTE: Teaming with unbelievers can weaken our integrity and commitment to what God wants us to do.

2 CORINTHIANS CHAPTER 7

CLEANSE YOURSELF

1 Having therefore these promises, beloved, let's cleanse ourselves from all defilement of flesh and spirit, perfecting holiness in the fear of God.

NOTE: We strive for perfection when we turn from sin and follow God's desires.

OPEN YOUR HEARTS TO THE TRUTH

2 Open your hearts to us. We wronged no one. We corrupted no one. We took advantage of no one.

2 CORINTHIANS CHAPTER 8

GIVE WHAT YOU CAN

11 But now complete the doing also, that as there was the readiness to be willing, so there may be the completion also out of your ability.

NOTE: Give enthusiastically, but give according to what you can give.

2 CORINTHIANS CHAPTER 9

BE A CHEERFUL GIVER

7 Let each man give according as he has determined in his heart, not grudgingly or under compulsion, for God loves a cheerful giver.

NOTE: The amount given is not as important as is giving enthusiastically from the heart.

2 CORINTHIANS CHAPTER 10

ONLY BOAST OF THE LORD

17 But "he who boasts, let him boast in the Lord."

2 CORINTHIANS CHAPTER 11

LISTEN

16 I say again, let no one think me foolish. But if so, yet receive me as foolish, that I also may boast a little.

NOTE: Paul is saying even if you think him foolish, listen to his wisdom and how he suffered for the Lord.

2 CORINTHIANS CHAPTER 13

PASS THE TEST OF GENUINE FAITH

5 Examine your own selves, whether you are in the faith. Test your own selves. Or don't you know about your own selves, that Jesus Christ is in you?—unless indeed you are disqualified.

NOTE: We should examine whether we are a true Christian or off-track.

GROW AS A CHRISTIAN

11 Finally, brothers, rejoice! Be perfected. Be comforted. Be of the same mind. Live in peace, and the God of love and peace will be with you.

12 Greet one another with a holy kiss.

THE COMMANDS OF GALATIANS

GALATIANS

GALATIANS CHAPTER 5

LOVE YOUR NEIGHBOR

1 Stand firm therefore in the liberty by which Christ has made us free, and don't be entangled again with a yoke of bondage.

NOTE: The yoke of bondage is becoming a slave to the law.

13 For you, brothers, were called for freedom. Only don't use your freedom for gain to the flesh, but through love be servants to one another.

NOTE: Use your freedom to serve others, not sin.

14 For the whole law is fulfilled in one word, in this: "You shall love your neighbor as yourself."

15 But if you bite and devour one another, be careful that you don't consume one another.

NOTE: Rather than fault-finding, lift each other up.

LET THE HOLY SPIRIT GUIDE YOUR LIFE

16 But I say, walk by the Spirit, and you won't fulfill the lust of the flesh.

25 If we live by the Spirit, let's also walk by the Spirit.

NOTE: The Spirit should lead every part of our lives.

AVOID BEING CONCEITED OR JEALOUS

26 Let's not become conceited, provoking one another, and envying one another.

NOTE: Seek God's approval, not the approval of men.

GALATIANS CHAPTER 6

GUIDE PEOPLE BACK TO THE PATH

1 Brothers, even if a man is caught in some fault, you who are spiritual must restore such a one in a spirit of gentleness; looking to yourself so that you also aren't tempted.

SHARE EACH OTHER'S TROUBLES AND PROBLEMS

2 Bear one another's burdens, and so fulfill the law of Christ.

DO YOUR VERY BEST AT YOUR WORK

4 But let each man examine his own work, and then he will have reason to boast in himself, and not in someone else.

PAY THOSE WHO TEACH YOU THE WORD

6 But let him who is taught in the word share all good things with him who teaches.

NOTE: Teachers should receive help for their physical and financial needs.

YOU REAP WHAT YOU SOW

7 Don't be deceived. God is not mocked, for whatever a man sows, that he will also reap.

DO WHAT IS RIGHT AND GOOD

9 Let's not be weary in doing good, for we will reap in due season, if we don't give up.

10 So then, as we have opportunity, let's do what is good toward all men, and especially toward those who are of the household of the faith.

THE COMMANDS
OF EPHESIANS

EPHESIANS

EPHESIANS CHAPTER 2

REMEMBER YOUR PAST

11 Therefore remember that once you, the Gentiles in the flesh, who are called "uncircumcision" by that which is called "circumcision" (in the flesh, made by hands),

12 that you were at that time separate from Christ, alienated from the commonwealth of Israel, and strangers from the covenants of the promise, having no hope and without God in the world.

NOTE: Gentiles are to be humble and thankful for their salvation.

EPHESIANS CHAPTER 4

STOP SINNING

17 This I say therefore, and testify in the Lord, that you no longer walk as the rest of the Gentiles also walk, in the futility of their mind,

22 that you put away, as concerning your former way of life, the old man that grows corrupt after the lusts of deceit,

BECOME A NEW PERSON

23 and that you be renewed in the spirit of your mind,

24 and put on the new man, who in the likeness of God has been created in righteousness and holiness of truth.

NOTE: Throw away your sinful desires and let the Spirit renew your mind to become like God.

STOP LYING

25 Therefore putting away falsehood, speak truth each one with his neighbor. For we are members of one another.

DON'T LET ANGER CONTROL YOU

26 "Be angry, and don't sin." Don't let the sun go down on your wrath,

27 and don't give place to the devil.

STOP STEALING

28 Let him who stole steal no more; but rather let him labor, producing with his hands something that is good, that he may have something to give to him who has need.

DON'T USE ABUSIVE LANGUAGE

29 Let no corrupt speech proceed out of your mouth, but only what is good for building others up as the need may be, that it may give grace to those who hear.

30 Don't grieve the Holy Spirit of God, in whom you were sealed for the day of redemption.

31 Let all bitterness, wrath, anger, outcry, and slander be put away from you, with all malice.

32 And be kind to one another, tender hearted, forgiving each other, just as God also in Christ forgave you.

EPHESIANS CHAPTER 5

FOLLOW GOD IN EVERYTHING

1 Be therefore imitators of God, as beloved children.

2 Walk in love, even as Christ also loved us and gave himself up for us, an offering and a sacrifice to God for a sweet-smelling fragrance.

NOTE: To imitate God is to follow God.

AVOID IMMORALITY AND FOOLISH TALK

3 But sexual immorality, and all uncleanness or covetousness, let it not even be mentioned among you, as becomes saints;

4 nor filthiness, nor foolish talking, nor jesting, which are not appropriate, but rather giving of thanks.

NOTE: Christians should not participate in improper, obscene jokes and stories.

DON'T EXCUSE SINS

6 Let no one deceive you with empty words. For because of these things, the wrath of God comes on the children of disobedience.

NOTE: No one should tell you sin is okay.

7 Therefore don't be partakers with them.

LIVE IN THE LIGHT

8 For you were once darkness, but are now light in the Lord. Walk as children of light,

9 for the fruit of the Spirit is in all goodness and righteousness and truth,

10 proving what is well pleasing to the Lord.

11 Have no fellowship with the unfruitful deeds of darkness, but rather even reprove them.

NOTE: To reprove is to expose evil deeds.

14 Therefore he says, "Awake, you who sleep, and arise from the dead, and Christ will shine on you."

15 Therefore watch carefully how you walk, not as unwise, but as wise,

17 Therefore don't be foolish, but understand what the will of the Lord is.

NO DRUNKENNESS

18 Don't be drunken with wine, in which is dissipation, but be filled with the Spirit,

NOTE: Drunkenness can ruin your life.

SING SONGS TO GOD

19 speaking to one another in psalms, hymns, and spiritual songs; singing and making melody in your heart to the Lord;

GIVE THANKS TO GOD

20 giving thanks always concerning all things in the name of our Lord Jesus Christ, to God, even the Father;

SUBMIT TO ONE ANOTHER

21 subjecting yourselves to one another in the fear of Christ.

22 Wives, be subject to your own husbands, as to the Lord.

23 For the husband is the head of the wife, as Christ also is the head of the assembly, being himself the savior of the body.

24 But as the assembly is subject to Christ, so let the wives also be to their own husbands in everything.

25 Husbands, love your wives, even as Christ also loved the assembly, and gave himself up for it;

26 that he might sanctify it, having cleansed it by the washing of water with the word,

27 that he might present the assembly to himself gloriously, not having spot or wrinkle or any such thing; but that it should be holy and without defect.

28 Even so husbands also ought to love their own wives as their own bodies. He who loves his own wife loves himself.

33 Nevertheless each of you must also love his own wife even as himself; and let the wife see that she respects her husband.

NOTE: Jesus died on the Christ to cleanse the church, and God's word cleanses people.

EPHESIANS CHAPTER 6

OBEY YOUR PARENTS

1 Children, obey your parents in the Lord, for this is right.

2 "Honor your father and mother," which is the first commandment with a promise:

3 "that it may be well with you, and you may live long on the earth."

RAISE CHILDREN WITH LOVING DISCIPLINE

4 You fathers, don't provoke your children to wrath, but nurture them in the discipline and instruction of the Lord.

SLAVES AND SLAVE OWNERS

5 Servants, be obedient to those who according to the flesh are your masters, with fear and trembling, in singleness of your heart, as to Christ,

9 You masters, do the same things to them, and give up threatening, knowing that he who is both their Master and yours is in heaven, and there is no partiality with him.

PUT ON GOD'S ARMOR

10 Finally, be strong in the Lord, and in the strength of his might.

11 Put on the whole armor of God, that you may be able to stand against the wiles of the devil.

12 For our wrestling is not against flesh and blood, but against the principalities, against the powers, against the world's rulers of the darkness of this age, and against the spiritual forces of wickedness in the heavenly places.

NOTE: We need spiritual, supernatural power that comes from God to defeat Satan.

13 Therefore put on the whole armor of God, that you may be able to withstand in the evil day, and having done all, to stand.

14 Stand therefore, having the utility belt of truth buckled around your waist, and having put on the breastplate of righteousness,

15 and having fitted your feet with the preparation of the Good News of peace,

16 above all, taking up the shield of faith, with which you will be able to quench all the fiery darts of the evil one.

17 And take the helmet of salvation, and the sword of the Spirit, which is the word of God;

18 with all prayer and requests, praying at all times in the Spirit, and being watchful to this end in all perseverance and requests for all the saints:

NOTE: The armor of God includes truth from God, righteousness, peace, faith, salvation, and the word of God, as well as the commandment to pray at all times.

THE COMMANDS
OF PHILIPPIANS

PHILIPPIANS

PHILIPPIANS CHAPTER 1

LIVE AS A CITIZEN OF HEAVEN

27 Only let your way of life be worthy of the Good News of Christ, that whether I come and see you or am absent, I may hear of your state, that you stand firm in one spirit, with one soul striving for the faith of the Good News;

DON'T BE INTIMIDATED BY YOUR ENEMIES

28 and in nothing frightened by the adversaries, which is for them a proof of destruction, but to you of salvation, and that from God.

PHILLIPPIANS CHAPTER 2

ENCOURAGE EACH OTHER

1 If therefore there is any exhortation in Christ, if any consolation of love, if any fellowship of the Spirit, if any tender mercies and compassion,

2 make my joy full by being like-minded, having the same love, being of one accord, of one mind;

NOTE: We should love one another in unity and with the same purpose.

BE HUMBLE

3 doing nothing through rivalry or through conceit, but in humility, each counting others better than himself;

4 each of you not just looking to his own things, but each of you also to the things of others.

LIVE LIKE JESUS

5 Have this in your mind, which was also in Christ Jesus,

6 who, existing in the form of God, didn't consider equality with God a thing to be grasped,

7 but emptied himself, taking the form of a servant, being made in the likeness of men.

8 And being found in human form, he humbled himself, becoming obedient to the point of death, yes, the death of the cross.

NOTE: We should humble ourselves as Jesus did, be servants, and obey God.

WORK HARD

12 So then, my beloved, even as you have always obeyed, not only in my presence, but now much more in my absence, work out your own salvation with fear and trembling.

DON'T ARGUE

14 Do all things without complaining and arguing…

HOLD FIRMLY TO THE WORD

16 holding up the word of life, that I may have something to boast in the day of Christ, that I didn't run in vain nor labor in vain.

NOTE: Live the word of God and live for God.

29 Receive him therefore in the Lord with all joy, and hold such people in honor…

PHILLIPPIANS CHAPTER 3

BE GLAD IN THE LORD

1 Finally, my brothers, rejoice in the Lord! To write the same things to you, to me indeed is not tiresome, but for you it is safe.

CIRCUMCISION

2 Beware of the dogs; beware of the evil workers; beware of the false circumcision

NOTE: Here, dogs mean those people who say you must be circumcised.

BE A MATURE CHRISTIAN

15 Let us therefore, as many as are perfect, think this way. If in anything you think otherwise, God will also reveal that to you.

16 Nevertheless, to the extent that we have already attained, let's walk by the same rule. Let's be of the same mind.

17 Brothers, be imitators together of me, and note those who walk this way, even as you have us for an example.

NOTE: Each Christian should strive to be perfect and mature and make progress to receive heavenly rewards.

PHILLIPPIANS CHAPTER 4

STAY TRUE TO THE LORD

1 Therefore, my brothers, beloved and longed for, my joy and crown, stand firm in the Lord in this way, my beloved.

BE FULL OF JOY

4 Rejoice in the Lord always! Again I will say, "Rejoice!"

BE UNSELFISH

5 Let your gentleness be known to all men. The Lord is at hand.

DON'T WORRY

6 In nothing be anxious, but in everything, by prayer and petition with thanksgiving, let your requests be made known to God.

FOCUS ON WHAT IS TRUE AND PURE

8 Finally, brothers, whatever things are true, whatever things are honorable, whatever things are just, whatever things are pure, whatever things are lovely, whatever things are of good report: if there is any virtue and if there is any praise, think about these things.

9 The things which you learned, received, heard, and saw in me: do these things, and the God of peace will be with you.

21 Greet every saint in Christ Jesus. The brothers who are with me greet you.

THE COMMANDS
OF COLOSSIANS

COLOSSIANS

COLOSSIANS CHAPTER 2

FOLLOW JESUS

6 As therefore you received Christ Jesus, the Lord, walk in him...

AVOID HUMAN THINKING

8 Be careful that you don't let anyone rob you through his philosophy and vain deceit, after the tradition of men, after the elements of the world, and not after Christ.

16 Let no one therefore judge you in eating, or in drinking, or with respect to a feast day or a new moon or a Sabbath day,

17 which are a shadow of the things to come; but the body is Christ's.

18 Let no one rob you of your prize by self-abasement and worshiping of the angels, dwelling in the things which he has not seen, vainly puffed up by his fleshly mind…

NOTE: Focus on Jesus Christ. Human traditions, philosophies, vanity, and the worshipping of angels can distract a person.

COLOSSIANS CHAPTER 3

FOCUS ON HEAVEN

1 If then you were raised together with Christ, seek the things that are above, where Christ is, seated on the right hand of God.

2 Set your mind on the things that are above, not on the things that are on the earth.

DEADEN YOURSELF TO SIN

5 Put to death therefore your members which are on the earth: sexual immorality, uncleanness, depraved passion, evil desire, and covetousness, which is idolatry.

NOTE: Avoid sinful, earthly desires, including sex outside of marriage and greed.

GET RID OF ANGER

8 ...but now you also put them all away: anger, wrath, malice, slander, and shameful speaking out of your mouth.

NOTE: Malice means, "ill will" or wishing bad things for someone.

DON'T LIE

9 Don't lie to one another, seeing that you have put off the old man with his doings,

BE KIND

12 Put on therefore, as God's chosen ones, holy and beloved, a heart of compassion, kindness, lowliness, humility, and perseverance;

FORGIVE

13 bearing with one another, and forgiving each other, if any man has a complaint against any; even as Christ forgave you, so you also do.

LOVE

14 Above all these things, walk in love, which is the bond of perfection.

LIVE IN PEACE

15 And let the peace of God rule in your hearts, to which also you were called in one body, and be thankful.

BE WISE, SING TO GOD

16 Let the word of Christ dwell in you richly; in all wisdom teaching and admonishing one another with psalms, hymns, and spiritual songs, singing with grace in your heart to the Lord.

REPRESENT JESUS

17 Whatever you do, in word or in deed, do all in the name of the Lord Jesus, giving thanks to God the Father, through him.

WIVES SUBMIT

18 Wives, be in subjection to your husbands, as is fitting in the Lord.

HUSBANDS SUBMIT

19 Husbands, love your wives, and don't be bitter against them.

CHILDREN OBEY

20 Children, obey your parents in all things, for this pleases the Lord.

USE FAIR DISCIPLINE

21 Fathers, don't provoke your children, so that they won't be discouraged.

SLAVES OBEY

22 Servants, obey in all things those who are your masters according to the flesh, not just when they are looking, as men pleasers, but in singleness of heart, fearing God.

WORK HARD

23 And whatever you do, work heartily, as for the Lord, and not for men,

COLOSSIANS CHAPTER 4

SLAVE OWNERS

1 Masters, give to your servants that which is just and equal, knowing that you also have a Master in heaven.

PRAY

2 Continue steadfastly in prayer, watching in it with thanksgiving,

3 praying together for us also, that God may open to us a door for the word, to speak the mystery of Christ, for which I am also in bonds…

SHARE THE GOOD NEWS

5 Walk in wisdom toward those who are outside, redeeming the time.

NOTE: Those "who are outside" refers to unbelievers.

CONVERSATION SHOULD BE GRACIOUS

6 Let your speech always be with grace, seasoned with salt, that you may know how you ought to answer each one.

NOTE: Our speech should be respectful, and the right tone should be used.

CARRY OUT THE MINISTRY

17 Tell Archippus, "Take heed to the ministry which you have received in the Lord, that you fulfill it."

NOTE: Paul's letter includes instruction for staying on track and fulfilling the ministry's needs.

THE COMMANDS
OF 1 THESSALONIANS

1 THESSALONIANS

1 THESSALONIANS CHAPTER 4

AVOID SEXUAL SIN

3 For this is the will of God: your sanctification, that you abstain from sexual immorality,

4 that each one of you know how to control his own body in sanctification and honor,

5 not in the passion of lust, even as the Gentiles who don't know God,

6 that no one should take advantage of and wrong a brother or sister in this matter; because the Lord is an avenger in all these things, as also we forewarned you and testified.

NOTE: God punishes those who sexually take advantage of others.

LIVE A QUIET LIFE

11 ...and that you make it your ambition to lead a quiet life, and to do your own business, and to work with your own hands, even as we instructed you;

12 that you may walk properly toward those who are outside, and may have need of nothing.

18 Therefore comfort one another with these words.

NOTE: God wants us to live quiet, hard-working lives so we are less dependent on others.

1 THESSALONIANS CHAPTER 5

STAY ALERT

6 ...so then let's not sleep, as the rest do, but let's watch and be sober.

8 But since we belong to the day, let's be sober, putting on the breastplate of faith and love, and for a helmet, the hope of salvation.

ENCOURAGE EACH OTHER

11 Therefore exhort one another, and build each other up, even as you also do.

12 But we beg you, brothers, to know those who labor among you, and are over you in the Lord, and admonish you,

NOTE: Show appreciation for church leaders and those who work with you.

ENCOURAGE THE LAZY, FRIGHTENED AND WEAK

13 and to respect and honor them in love for their work's sake.

14 We exhort you, brothers: Admonish the disorderly; encourage the faint-hearted; support the weak; be patient toward all.

NOTE: Be patient with people, but warn the lazy and lift up the weaker, fearful people.

DON'T REPAY EVIL

15 See that no one returns evil for evil to anyone, but always follow after that which is good for one another and for all.

BE JOYFUL

16 Always rejoice.

ALWAYS PRAY

17 Pray without ceasing.

BE THANKFUL

18 In everything give thanks, for this is the will of God in Christ Jesus toward you.

DON'T SMOTHER THE HOLY SPIRIT

19 Don't quench the Spirit.

NOTE: Fully support the working of the Holy Spirit in a person's life.

DON'T SCOFF AT PROPHECIES

20 Don't despise prophecies.

TEST EVERYTHING

21 Test all things, and hold firmly that which is good.

NOTE: We test things using God's words from the Bible.

STAY AWAY FROM EVIL

22 Abstain from every form of evil.

GREET WITH A KISS

26 Greet all the brothers with a holy kiss.

READ THIS LETTER

27 I solemnly command you by the Lord that this letter be read to all the holy brothers.

THE COMMANDS
OF 2 THESSALONIANS

2 THESSALONIANS

2 THESSALONIANS CHAPTER 1

GOD PROVIDES REST

7 ...and to give relief to you who are afflicted with us, when the Lord Jesus is revealed from heaven with his mighty angels in flaming fire...

NOTE: It is joyous to understand that we will one day stand before Jesus despite our suffering.

2 THESSALONIANS CHAPTER 2

DON'T BE FOOLED BY THE DAY OF THE LORD'S ARRIVAL

2 ...not to be quickly shaken in your mind, and not be troubled, either by spirit, or by word, or by letter as if from us, saying that the day of Christ has already come.

3 Let no one deceive you in any way. For it will not be, unless the rebellion comes first, and the man of sin is revealed, the son of destruction...

NOTE: Many will falsely predict the time Jesus will return.

STAND FIRM TO THE TRUTH

15 So then, brothers, stand firm and hold the traditions which you were taught by us, whether by word or by letter.

2 THESSALONIANS CHAPTER 3

PRAY FOR THE LORD'S MESSAGE

1 Finally, brothers, pray for us, that the word of the Lord may spread rapidly and be glorified, even as also with you...

STAY AWAY FROM LAZY BELIEVERS

6 Now we command you, brothers, in the name of our Lord Jesus Christ, that you withdraw yourselves from every brother who walks in rebellion, and not after the tradition which they received from us.

10 For even when we were with you, we commanded you this: "If anyone is not willing to work, don't let him eat."

11 For we hear of some who walk among you in rebellion, who don't work at all, but are busybodies.

12 Now those who are that way, we command and exhort in the Lord Jesus Christ, that they work with quietness and eat their own bread.

13 But you, brothers, don't be weary in doing what is right.

14 If any man doesn't obey our word in this letter, note that man, that you have no company with him, to the end that he may be ashamed.

15 Don't count him as an enemy, but admonish him as a brother.

NOTE: Believers should avoid laziness, be hard-working, and avoid those people walking in rebellion.

THE COMMANDS OF 1 TIMOTHY

1 TIMOTHY

1 TIMOTHY CHAPTER 1

DON'T WASTE TIME IN MEANINGLESS DISCUSSION

3 As I urged you when I was going into Macedonia, stay at Ephesus that you might command certain men not to teach a different doctrine,

4 and not to pay attention to myths and endless genealogies, which cause disputes, rather than God's stewardship, which is in faith—

NOTE: Focus on truthful teachings and faith in God.

BE FILLED WITH LOVE

5 but the goal of this command is love, out of a pure heart and a good conscience and sincere faith...

FIGHT WELL IN THE LORD'S BATTLES

18 I commit this instruction to you, my child Timothy, according to the prophecies which were given to you before, that by them you may wage the good warfare,

NOTE: Paul encourages Timothy to fight the battles of the Lord, which we should also do.

CLING TIGHTLY TO YOUR FAITH

19 holding faith and a good conscience, which some having thrust away made a shipwreck concerning the faith,

NOTE: By focusing on faith, believers can live with a clear conscience.

1 TIMOTHY CHAPTER 2

PRAY FOR THE PEOPLE

1 I exhort therefore, first of all, that petitions, prayers, intercessions, and givings of thanks be made for all men:

2 for kings and all who are in high places, that we may lead a tranquil and quiet life in all godliness and reverence.

NOTE: Believers should pray for all people.

PRAY WITH HANDS LIFTED

8 I desire therefore that the men in every place pray, lifting up holy hands without anger and doubting.

WOMEN DRESS APPROPRIATELY

9 In the same way, that women also adorn themselves in decent clothing, with modesty and propriety, not just with braided hair, gold, pearls, or expensive clothing,

WOMEN DON'T TEACH MEN

11 Let a woman learn in quietness with full submission.

12 But I don't permit a woman to teach, nor to exercise authority over a man, but to be in quietness.

1 TIMOTHY CHAPTER 3

ELDER/PASTOR REQUIREMENTS

1 This is a faithful saying: someone who seeks to be an overseer desires a good work.

NOTE: Overseer is a church leader or elder.

2 The overseer therefore must be without reproach, the husband of one wife, temperate, sensible, modest, hospitable, good at teaching;

3 not a drinker, not violent, not greedy for money, but gentle, not quarrelsome, not covetous;

4 one who rules his own house well, having children in subjection with all reverence;

5 (but how could someone who doesn't know how to rule one's own house take care of God's assembly?)

6 not a new convert, lest being puffed up he fall into the same condemnation as the devil.

NOTE: Elders should be mature in their faith.

7 Moreover he must have good testimony from those who are outside, to avoid falling into reproach and the snare of the devil.

NOTE: Even people outside the church should speak well of the elder.

8 Servants, in the same way, must be reverent, not double-tongued, not addicted to much wine, not greedy for money,

NOTE: Servants here refers to Deacons.

9 holding the mystery of the faith in a pure conscience.

10 Let them also first be tested; then let them serve if they are blameless.

11 Their wives in the same way must be reverent, not slanderers, temperate, and faithful in all things.

12 Let servants be husbands of one wife, ruling their children and their own houses well.

13 For those who have served well gain for themselves a good standing, and great boldness in the faith which is in Christ Jesus.

1 TIMOTHY CHAPTER 4

DON'T WASTE TIME ARGUING

7 But refuse profane and old wives' fables. Exercise yourself toward godliness.

NOTE: Focus on the word of God, not secular fables.

11 Command and teach these things.

BE AN EXAMPLE

12. Let no man despise your youth; but be an example to those who believe, in word, in your way of life, in love, in spirit, in faith, and in purity.

READ SCRIPTURE TO THE CHURCH

13 Until I come, pay attention to reading, to exhortation, and to teaching.

USE YOUR SPIRITUAL GIFTS

14 Don't neglect the gift that is in you, which was given to you by prophecy, with the laying on of the hands of the elders.

BE TASK FOCUSED

15 Be diligent in these things. Give yourself wholly to them, that your progress may be revealed to all.

WATCH HOW YOU LIVE

16 Pay attention to yourself and to your teaching. Continue in these things, for in doing this you will save both yourself and those who hear you.

NOTE: The church requires mature widows because younger widows may be distracted by marriage.

1 TIMOTHY CHAPTER 5

TREAT OLDER MEN WELL

1 Don't rebuke an older man, but exhort him as a father; the younger men as brothers;

TREAT OLDER WOMEN WELL

2 the elder women as mothers; the younger as sisters, in all purity.

TAKE CARE OF WIDOWS

3 Honor widows who are widows indeed.

4 But if any widow has children or grandchildren, let them learn first to show piety toward their own family and to repay their parents, for this is acceptable in the sight of God.

NOTE: Children and grandchildren should help take care of widows.

7 Also command these things, that they may be without reproach.

WIDOWS AS CHURCH WORKERS

9 Let no one be enrolled as a widow under sixty years old, having been the wife of one man,

10 being approved by good works, if she has brought up children, if she has been hospitable to strangers, if she has washed the saints' feet, if she has relieved the afflicted, and if she has diligently followed every good work.

11 But refuse younger widows, for when they have grown wanton against Christ, they desire to marry,

16 If any man or woman who believes has widows, let them relieve them, and don't let the assembly be burdened, that it might relieve those who are widows indeed.

NOTE: The church requires mature widows because younger widows may be distracted by marriage and the things of this world.

ELDERS SHOULD BE PAID WELL

17 Let the elders who rule well be counted worthy of double honor, especially those who labor in the word and in teaching.

18 For the Scripture says, "You shall not muzzle the ox when it treads out the grain." And, "The laborer is worthy of his wages."

NOTE: An elder should be paid well.

ELDER DISCIPLINE

19 Don't receive an accusation against an elder, except at the word of two or three witnesses.

20 Those who sin, reprove in the sight of all, that the rest also may be in fear.

SHOW NO FAVORITISM

21 I command you in the sight of God, and the Lord Jesus Christ, and the chosen angels, that you observe these things without prejudice, doing nothing by partiality.

22 Lay hands hastily on no one. Don't be a participant in other people's sins. Keep yourself pure.

NOTE: Don't be in a hurry to approve someone not qualified.

WINE FOR MEDICINE

23 Be no longer a drinker of water only, but use a little wine for your stomach's sake and your frequent infirmities.

1 TIMOTHY CHAPTER 6

SLAVES SHOW FULL RESPECT

1 Let as many as are bondservants under the yoke count their own masters worthy of all honor, that the name of God and the doctrine not be blasphemed.

NOTE: Servants should respect their masters.

2 Those who have believing masters, let them not despise them because they are brothers, but rather let them serve them, because those who partake of the benefit are believing and beloved. Teach and exhort these things.

NOTE: Masters who are believers should treat slaves with respect, which helps other believers.

WHOLESOME TEACHING PROMOTES GODLY LIFE

3 If anyone teaches a different doctrine, and doesn't consent to sound words, the words of our Lord Jesus Christ, and to the doctrine which is according to godliness,

BE WARY OF GODLESS TEACHING

4 he is conceited, knowing nothing, but obsessed with arguments, disputes, and word battles, from which come envy, strife, insulting, evil suspicions,

5 constant friction of people of corrupt minds and destitute of the truth, who suppose that godliness is a means of gain. Withdraw yourself from such.

NOTE: Avoid those who want to argue over words and stir up arguments.

BE CONTENT WITH FOOD AND CLOTHING

8 But having food and clothing, we will be content with that.

MONEY IS THE ROOT OF ALL EVIL

9 But those who are determined to be rich fall into a temptation, a snare, and many foolish and harmful lusts, such as drown men in ruin and destruction.

10 For the love of money is a root of all kinds of evil. Some have been led astray from the faith in their greed, and have pierced themselves through with many sorrows.

NOTE: Greed can bring destruction.

RUN FROM EVIL

11 But you, man of God, flee these things, and follow after righteousness, godliness, faith, love, perseverance, and gentleness.

FIGHT THE GOOD FIGHT FOR ETERNAL LIFE

12 Fight the good fight of faith. Take hold of the eternal life to which you were called, and you confessed the good confession in the sight of many witnesses.

OBEY COMMANDS WITHOUT WAVERING

14 that you keep the commandment without spot, blameless, until the appearing of our Lord Jesus Christ,

NOTE: Be sure to obey the Commands until Jesus comes back.

TRUST IN GOD, NOT MONEY

17 Charge those who are rich in this present world that they not be arrogant, nor have their hope set on the uncertainty of riches, but on the living God, who richly provides us with everything to enjoy;

18 that they do good, that they be rich in good works, that they be ready to distribute, willing to share;

19 laying up in store for themselves a good foundation against the time to come, that they may lay hold of eternal life.

AVOID FOOLISH DISCUSSIONS

20 Timothy, guard that which is committed to you, turning away from the empty chatter and oppositions of what is falsely called knowledge,

NOTE: Avoid Godless discussions.

THE COMMANDS
OF 2 TIMOTHY

2 TIMOTHY

2 TIMOTHY CHAPTER 1

BE STRONG AND BOLD

6 For this cause, I remind you that you should stir up the gift of God which is in you through the laying on of my hands.

NOTE: Paul wants Timothy to be bold in sharing the good news from God. Something all believers should learn from.

NEVER BE ASHAMED OF THE LORD

8 Therefore don't be ashamed of the testimony of our Lord, nor of me his prisoner; but endure hardship for the Good News according to the power of God…

HOLD ONTO TRUTHFUL TEACHING

13 Hold the pattern of sound words which you have heard from me, in faith and love which is in Christ Jesus.

GUARD THE TRUTH

14 That good thing which was committed to you, guard through the Holy Spirit who dwells in us.

2 TIMOTHY CHAPTER 2

BE STRONG WITH GRACE

1 You therefore, my child, be strengthened in the grace that is in Christ Jesus.

TEACH GREAT TRUTHS

2 The things which you have heard from me among many witnesses, commit the same things to faithful men, who will be able to teach others also.

ENDURE SUFFERING

3 You therefore must endure hardship as a good soldier of Christ Jesus.

FARMERS ENJOY FIRST FRUIT

6 The farmer who labors must be the first to get a share of the crops.

7 Consider what I say, and may the Lord give you understanding in all things.

PREACH THE GOOD NEWS

8 Remember Jesus Christ, risen from the dead, of the offspring of David, according to my Good News…

NOTE: The foundation of faith is that Jesus died on the cross for our sins and rose again.

STOP FIGHTING OVER WORDS

14 Remind them of these things, charging them in the sight of the Lord, that they don't argue about words, to no profit, to the subverting of those who hear.

NOTE: Quibbling over words or engaging in foolish discussion can take a believer off track.

WORK HARD

15 Give diligence to present yourself approved by God, a workman who doesn't need to be ashamed, properly handling the Word of Truth.

NOTE: God wants us to work hard on our duties and learn the word of God.

AVOID FOOLISH TALK

16 But shun empty chatter, for it will go further in ungodliness…

TURN FROM EVIL

19 However God's firm foundation stands, having this seal, "The Lord knows those who are his," and, "Let every one who names the name of the Lord depart from unrighteousness."

NOTE: Those who know God should depart from evil and wickedness.

RUN FROM LUST AND EVIL THOUGHTS

22 Flee from youthful lusts; but pursue righteousness, faith, love, and peace with those who call on the Lord out of a pure heart.

RUN FROM ARGUMENTS

23 But refuse foolish and ignorant questionings, knowing that they generate strife.

BE GENTLE AND KIND

24 The Lord's servant must not quarrel, but be gentle toward all, able to teach, patient,

GENTLY INSTRUCT THOSE WHO OPPOSE THE TRUTH

25 in gentleness correcting those who oppose him: perhaps God may give them repentance leading to a full knowledge of the truth,

2 TIMOTHY CHAPTER 3

STAY AWAY FROM SCOFFERS

1 But know this: that in the last days, grievous times will come.

2 For men will be lovers of self, lovers of money, boastful, arrogant, blasphemers, disobedient to parents, unthankful, unholy,

3 without natural affection, unforgiving, slanderers, without self-control, fierce, not lovers of good,

4 traitors, headstrong, conceited, lovers of pleasure rather than lovers of God,

5 holding a form of godliness, but having denied its power. Turn away from these, also.

NOTE: The outer appearance of Christian traditions does not equal inner belief and loving others.

REMAIN FAITHFUL TO THE TEACHING

14 But you remain in the things which you have learned and have been assured of, knowing from whom you have learned them.

2 TIMOTHY CHAPTER 4

PREACH THE WORD, IN SEASON OR OUT

2 preach the word; be urgent in season and out of season; reprove, rebuke, and exhort with all patience and teaching.

CARRY OUT THE MINISTRY

5 But you be sober in all things, suffer hardship, do the work of an evangelist, and fulfill your ministry.

NOTE: You will suffer for God, but you must continue to share the good news of Jesus Christ.

THE COMMANDS
OF TITUS

TITUS

TITUS CHAPTER 1

ELDER REQUIREMENTS

6 ...if anyone is blameless, the husband of one wife, having children who believe, who are not accused of loose or unruly behavior.

7 For the overseer must be blameless, as God's steward, not self-pleasing, not easily angered, not given to wine, not violent, not greedy for dishonest gain;

NOTE: An overseer is a church leader or Elder.

8 but given to hospitality, a lover of good, sober minded, fair, holy, self-controlled,

9 holding to the faithful word which is according to the teaching, that he may be able to exhort in the sound doctrine, and to convict those who contradict him.

NOTE: An elder should use God's word to encourage people and correct those who are wrong.

SILENCE THOSE WHO REFUSE TO OBEY

11 ...whose mouths must be stopped: men who overthrow whole houses, teaching things which they ought not, for dishonest gain's sake.

13 This testimony is true. For this cause, reprove them sharply, that they may be sound in the faith,

14 not paying attention to Jewish fables and commandments of men who turn away from the truth.

NOTE: Believers must follow the word of God, not myths or false teachers.

TITUS CHAPTER 2

PROMOTE RIGHT LIVING

1 But say the things which fit sound doctrine,

OLDER MEN REQUIREMENTS

2 that older men should be temperate, sensible, sober minded, sound in faith, in love, and in perseverance:

OLDER WOMEN REQUIREMENTS

3 and that older women likewise be reverent in behavior, not slanderers nor enslaved to much wine, teachers of that which is good,

YOUNGER WOMEN REQUIREMENTS

4 that they may train the young wives to love their husbands, to love their children,

5 to be sober minded, chaste, workers at home, kind, being in subjection to their own husbands, that God's word may not be blasphemed.

YOUNGER MEN REQUIREMENTS

6 Likewise, exhort the younger men to be sober minded.

BE AN EXAMPLE FOR OTHERS

7 In all things show yourself an example of good works. In your teaching, show integrity, seriousness, incorruptibility,

8 and soundness of speech that can't be condemned, that he who opposes you may be ashamed, having no evil thing to say about us.

SLAVE REQUIREMENTS

9 Exhort servants to be in subjection to their own masters and to be well-pleasing in all things, not contradicting,

10 not stealing, but showing all good fidelity, that they may adorn the doctrine of God, our Savior, in all things.

15 Say these things and exhort and reprove with all authority. Let no one despise you.

NOTE: Encourage and teach each other with the authority to correct other people.

TITUS CHAPTER 3

OBEY THE GOVERNMENT

1 Remind them to be in subjection to rulers and to authorities, to be obedient, to be ready for every good work,

AVOID SLANDER

2 to speak evil of no one, not to be contentious, to be gentle, showing all humility toward all men.

BE DEVOTED TO GOOD DEEDS

8 This saying is faithful, and concerning these things I desire that you affirm confidently, so that those who have believed God may be careful to maintain good works. These things are good and profitable to men;

AVOID QUARRELS OVER THEOLOGICAL IDEAS

9 but shun foolish questionings, genealogies, strife, and disputes about the law; for they are unprofitable and vain.

WARN DIVISIVE PEOPLE

10 Avoid a factious man after a first and second warning,

11 knowing that such a one is perverted and sins, being self-condemned.

NOTE: Believers must deal with those causing divisions.

HELP WITH THE URGENT NEEDS OF OTHERS

14 Let our people also learn to maintain good works for necessary uses, that they may not be unfruitful.

15 All who are with me greet you. Greet those who love us in faith. Grace be with you all. Amen.

THE COMMANDS
OF PHILEMON

PHILEMON

There are no Commands from Philemon. It is a letter from Paul while in prison (and also from Timothy) to Philemon and two other Christians, Apphia and Archippus. Paul appeals to Philemon on behalf of his son Onesimus, whom he is sending back to Philemon to be entirely accepted and welcomed. Paul also adds that he will pay whatever costs Onesimus incurs and further asks Philemon to prepare a guest room for Paul himself, hoping he will someday gain his freedom. The closest thing we get to a Command is to accept other Christians fully.

THE COMMANDS
OF HEBREWS

HEBREWS

HEBREWS CHAPTER 3

DON'T TURN FROM GOD

1 Therefore, holy brothers, partakers of a heavenly calling, consider the Apostle and High Priest of our confession: Jesus,

12 Beware, brothers, lest perhaps there might be in any one of you an evil heart of unbelief, in falling away from the living God;

13 but exhort one another day by day, so long as it is called "today", lest any one of you be hardened by the deceitfulness of sin.

15 while it is said, "Today if you will hear his voice, don't harden your hearts, as in the rebellion."

NOTE: Focus on Jesus and God; otherwise, you can fall into sin and rebellion and live with hardened hearts.

HEBREWS CHAPTER 4

FOCUS ON ENTERING THE PLACE OF REST

1 Let's fear therefore, lest perhaps anyone of you should seem to have come short of a promise of entering into his rest.

11 Let's therefore give diligence to enter into that rest, lest anyone fall after the same example of disobedience.

14 Having then a great high priest who has passed through the heavens, Jesus, the Son of God, let's hold tightly to our confession.

16 Let's therefore draw near with boldness to the throne of grace, that we may receive mercy and may find grace for help in time of need.

NOTE: Focus on obeying God and holding tightly to your beliefs; you will receive mercy and grace.

HEBREWS CHAPTER 6

BECOME MATURE IN UNDERSTANDING

1 Therefore leaving the teaching of the first principles of Christ, let's press on to perfection—not laying again a foundation of repentance from dead works, of faith toward God,

FOLLOW GOD'S EXAMPLES

12 ...that you won't be sluggish, but imitators of those who through faith and perseverance inherited the promises.

NOTE: Once you understand the basics of Jesus and teachings, strive to learn more, and you won't become indifferent or lazy.

HEBREWS CHAPTER 10

FULLY TRUST GOD

22 let's draw near with a true heart in fullness of faith, having our hearts sprinkled from an evil conscience, and having our body washed with pure water,

HOLD ONTO SALVATION

23 let's hold fast the confession of our hope without wavering; for he who promised is faithful.

MOTIVATE OTHERS TO LOVE AND KINDNESS

24 Let's consider how to provoke one another to love and good works,

NOTE: The blood of Christ and the cleansing of water open our hearts, strengthen our faith, and draw us closer to God. Follow this up with love and good deeds to help others.

MEET TOGETHER

25 not forsaking our own assembling together, as the custom of some is, but exhorting one another, and so much the more as you see the Day approaching.

KEEP YOUR TRUST IN THE LORD

35 Therefore don't throw away your boldness, which has a great reward.

NOTE: Boldness means trust in the Lord.

HEBREWS CHAPTER 11

IT'S IMPOSSIBLE TO PLEASE GOD WITHOUT FAITH

6 Without faith it is impossible to be well pleasing to him, for he who comes to God must believe that he exists, and that he is a rewarder of those who seek him.

HEBREWS CHAPTER 12

STRIP OFF SIN AND RUN YOUR RACE FOR GOD

1 Therefore let's also, seeing we are surrounded by so great a cloud of witnesses, lay aside every weight and the sin which so easily entangles us, and let's run with perseverance the race that is set before us,

KEEP YOUR EYES ON JESUS

2 looking to Jesus, the author and perfecter of faith, who for the joy that was set before him endured the cross, despising its shame, and has sat down at the right hand of the throne of God.

3 For consider him who has endured such contradiction of sinners against himself, that you don't grow weary, fainting in your souls.

NOTE: Remember the anger and suffering Jesus went through, so you don't give up.

ACCEPT THE LORD'S DISCIPLINE

5 You have forgotten the exhortation which reasons with you as with children, "My son, don't take lightly the chastening of the Lord, nor faint when you are reproved by him;

6 for whom the Lord loves, he disciplines, and chastises every son whom he receives."

NOTE: The Lord disciplines and punishes those he loves.

FOLLOW THE STRAIGHT PATH

12 Therefore lift up the hands that hang down and the feeble knees,

13 and make straight paths for your feet, so what is lame may not be dislocated, but rather be healed.

14 Follow after peace with all men, and the sanctification without which no man will see the Lord,

15 looking carefully lest there be any man who falls short of the grace of God, lest any root of bitterness springing up trouble you, and many be defiled by it...

NOTE: Even when tired or weak, mark a path for others to follow. Be at peace with everyone and allow no bitterness that brings resentment.

LISTEN AND OBEY

25 See that you don't refuse him who speaks. For if they didn't escape when they refused him who warned on the earth, how much more will we not escape who turn away from him who warns from heaven,

28 Therefore, receiving a Kingdom that can't be shaken, let's have grace, through which we serve God acceptably, with reverence and awe,

29 for our God is a consuming fire.

NOTE: The people of Israel did not listen to Moses and suffered; how much more if we

reject God in heaven? Instead, be thankful and worship God with both fear and awe.

HEBREWS CHAPTER 13

LOVE EACH OTHER

1 Let brotherly love continue.

2 Don't forget to show hospitality to strangers, for in doing so, some have entertained angels without knowing it.

3 Remember those who are in bonds, as bound with them, and those who are ill-treated, since you are also in the body.

NOTE: Have compassion for those in jail or prison as if you were there yourself.

DON'T LOVE MONEY

5 Be free from the love of money, content with such things as you have, for he has said, "I will in no way leave you, neither will I in any way forsake you."

FOLLOW THE EXAMPLE OF THOSE WHO TEACH THE WORD

7 Remember your leaders, men who spoke to you the word of God, and considering the results of their conduct, imitate their faith.

AVOID STRANGE IDEAS

9 Don't be carried away by various and strange teachings, for it is good that the heart be established by grace, not by food, through which those who were so occupied were not benefited.

BE A SACRIFICE FOR GOD

13 Let's therefore go out to him outside of the camp, bearing his reproach.

15 Through him, then, let's offer up a sacrifice of praise to God continually, that is, the fruit of lips which proclaim allegiance to his name

16 But don't forget to be doing good and sharing, for with such sacrifices God is well pleased.

OBEY SPIRITUAL LEADERS AND PRAY FOR THEM

17 Obey your leaders and submit to them, for they watch on behalf of your souls, as those who will give account, that they may do this with joy, and not with groaning, for that would be unprofitable for you.

18 Pray for us, for we are persuaded that we have a good conscience, desiring to live honorably in all things.

22 But I exhort you, brothers, endure the word of exhortation; for I have written to you in few words.

24 Greet all of your leaders and all the saints. The Italians greet you.

NOTE: To endure in verse 22 is to pay attention to the words written.

THE COMMANDS OF JAMES

JAMES

JAMES CHAPTER 1

CONSIDER TROUBLES A JOY

2 Count it all joy, my brothers, when you fall into various temptations,

BE PATIENT

4 Let endurance have its perfect work, that you may be perfect and complete, lacking in nothing.

SEEK WISDOM

5 But if any of you lacks wisdom, let him ask of God, who gives to all liberally and without reproach, and it will be given to him.

6 But let him ask in faith, without any doubting, for he who doubts is like a wave of the sea, driven by the wind and tossed.

NOTE: If you need wisdom, ask God without doubt and with faith, and it will be given to you.

GOD HONORS THE POOR

9 But let the brother in humble circumstances glory in his high position;

GOD HUMBLES THE RICH

10 and the rich, in that he is made humble, because like the flower in the grass, he will pass away.

NOTE: God honors the poor and humbles the rich.

GOD NEVER TEMPTS YOU TO DO WRONG

13 Let no man say when he is tempted, "I am tempted by God," for God can't be tempted by evil, and he himself tempts no one.

16 Don't be deceived, my beloved brothers.

BE QUICK TO LISTEN, SLOW TO SPEAK, SLOW TO ANGER

19 So, then, my beloved brothers, let every man be swift to hear, slow to speak, and slow to anger;

20 for the anger of man doesn't produce the righteousness of God.

GET RID OF ALL EVIL

21 Therefore, putting away all filthiness and overflowing of wickedness, receive with humility the implanted word, which is able to save your souls.

BE A DOER OF THE WORD

22 But be doers of the word, and not only hearers, deluding your own selves.

NOTE: A believer should not just listen to the word of God, but do what it says.

JAMES CHAPTER 2

DON'T FAVOR SOME PEOPLE OVER OTHERS

1 My brothers, don't hold the faith of our Lord Jesus Christ of glory with partiality.

REMEMBER, THE POOR INHERIT THE KINGDOM OF GOD

5 Listen, my beloved brothers. Didn't God choose those who are poor in this world to be rich in faith, and heirs of the Kingdom which he promised to those who love him?

NOTE: The poor are rich in faith and will inherit the Kingdom of God.

WATCH WHAT YOU SAY AND DO

11 For he who said, "Do not commit adultery," also said, "Do not commit murder." Now if you do not commit adultery, but murder, you have become a transgressor of the law.

12 So speak and so do, as men who are to be judged by a law of freedom.

NOTE: We are judged by the same law that sets us free.

JAMES CHAPTER 3

CHURCH TEACHERS ARE JUDGED STRICTLY

1 Let not many of you be teachers, my brothers, knowing that we will receive heavier judgment.

AVOID BLESSING AND CURSES FROM THE SAME MOUTH

10 Out of the same mouth comes blessing and cursing. My brothers, these things ought not to be so.

LIVE HONORABLY AND DO GOOD WORKS

13 Who is wise and understanding among you? Let him show by his good conduct that his deeds are done in gentleness of wisdom.

AVOID JEALOUSY AND SELFISHNESS

14 But if you have bitter jealousy and selfish ambition in your heart, don't boast and don't lie against the truth.

JAMES CHAPTER 4

RESIST THE DEVIL, AND HE WILL FLEE

7 Be subject therefore to God. Resist the devil, and he will flee from you.

COME CLOSER TO GOD, AND HE COMES CLOSER TO YOU

8 Draw near to God, and he will draw near to you. Cleanse your hands, you sinners. Purify your hearts, you double-minded.

DIVIDED LOYALTY LEADS TO SORROW

9 Lament, mourn, and weep. Let your laughter be turned to mourning, and your joy to gloom.

10 Humble yourselves in the sight of the Lord, and he will exalt you.

DON'T CRITICIZE AND JUDGE OTHERS

11 Don't speak against one another, brothers. He who speaks against a brother and judges his brother, speaks against the law and judges the law. But if you judge the law, you are not a doer of the law, but a judge.

SEEK WHAT THE LORD WANTS

13 Come now, you who say, "Today or tomorrow let's go into this city, and spend a year there, trade, and make a profit."

14 Whereas you don't know what your life will be like tomorrow. For what is your life? For you are a vapor that appears for a little time, and then vanishes away.

15 For you ought to say, "If the Lord wills, we will both live, and do this or that."

NOTE: We may make plans, but it is better to say, "if God is willing" or "if God wants us to," for God has his plans for us.

JAMES CHAPTER 5

THE RICH WILL WEEP AND GROAN

1 Come now, you rich, weep and howl for your miseries that are coming on you.

BE PATIENT AND WAIT FOR THE LORD'S RETURN

7 Be patient therefore, brothers, until the coming of the Lord. Behold, the farmer waits for the precious fruit of the earth, being patient over it, until it receives the early and late rain.

8 You also be patient. Establish your hearts, for the coming of the Lord is at hand.

9 Don't grumble, brothers, against one another, so that you won't be judged. Behold, the judge stands at the door.

NOTE: To grumble is to complain.

10 Take, brothers, for an example of suffering and of perseverance, the prophets who spoke in the name of the Lord.

DO NOT SWEAR OR TAKE AN OATH

12 But above all things, my brothers, don't swear— not by heaven, or by the earth, or by any other oath; but let your "yes" be "yes", and your "no", "no", so that you don't fall into hypocrisy.

PRAY DURING HARDSHIPS

13 Is any among you suffering? Let him pray. Is any cheerful? Let him sing praises.

NOTE: Pray when you are suffering, sing when you are happy.

ANOINT THE SICK WITH OIL AND PRAY

14 Is any among you sick? Let him call for the elders of the assembly, and let them pray over him, anointing him with oil in the name of the Lord,

CONFESS YOUR SINS TO EACH OTHER

16 Confess your offenses to one another, and pray for one another, that you may be healed. The insistent prayer of a righteous person is powerfully effective.

THE COMMANDS
OF 1 PETER

I PETER

I PETER CHAPTER 1

USE SELF-CONTROL

13 Therefore prepare your minds for action. Be sober, and set your hope fully on the grace that will be brought to you at the revelation of Jesus Christ—

BE OBEDIENT

14 as children of obedience, not conforming yourselves according to your former lusts as in your ignorance,

BE HOLY

15 but just as he who called you is holy, you yourselves also be holy in all of your behavior;

16 because it is written, "You shall be holy; for I am holy."

YOU ARE JUDGED ON WHAT YOU DO

17 If you call on him as Father, who without respect of persons judges according to each man's work, pass the time of your living as foreigners here in reverent fear,

NOTE: God does not want you to play favorites, he judges a person by their actions.

REMEMBER GOD PAID TO SAVE YOU

18 knowing that you were redeemed, not with corruptible things, with silver or gold, from the useless way of life handed down from your fathers,

NOTE: Jesus shed his blood on the cross to save believers.

CLEANSE YOUR SINS BY OBEYING THE TRUTH

22 Seeing you have purified your souls in your obedience to the truth through the Spirit in sincere brotherly affection, love one another from the heart fervently,

NOTE: Since your souls are cleansed by obeying the truth, love one another with all your heart.

I PETER CHAPTER 2

GET RID OF HATRED

1 Putting away therefore all wickedness, all deceit, hypocrisies, envies, and all evil speaking,

CRAVE PURE SPIRITUAL MILK

2 as newborn babies, long for the pure milk of the Word, that with it you may grow...

NOTE: The word of God will help you grow as a believer.

AVOID WORLDLY DESIRES

11 Beloved, I beg you as foreigners and pilgrims, to abstain from fleshly lusts, which war against the soul;

NOTE: Earthly desires can destroy our souls, so our focus should be on God and our future in heaven.

BEHAVE WELL AROUND UNBELIEVERS

12 ...having good behavior among the nations, so in that of which they speak against you as evildoers, they may by your good works, which they see, glorify God in the day of visitation.

NOTE: A believer's behavior can influence unbelievers by living a Christian life; at judgment, the unbeliever will praise God.

SUBMIT TO AUTHORITY

13 Therefore subject yourselves to every ordinance of man for the Lord's sake: whether to the king, as supreme;

NOTE: A believer should submit to human authority as well as the authority of God.

RESPECT EVERYONE

17 Honor all men. Love the brotherhood. Fear God. Honor the king.

SLAVES SUBMIT TO MASTERS

18 Servants, be in subjection to your masters with all respect: not only to the good and gentle, but also to the wicked.

I PETER CHAPTER 3

WIVES ACCEPT YOUR HUSBANDS PLANS

1 In the same way, wives, be in subjection to your own husbands; so that, even if any don't obey the Word, they may be won by the behavior of their wives without a word…

FOCUS ON THE BEAUTY WITHIN

3 Let your beauty be not just the outward adorning of braiding the hair, and of wearing jewels of gold, or of putting on fine clothing;

4 but in the hidden person of the heart, in the incorruptible adornment of a gentle and quiet spirit, which is very precious in the sight of God.

NOTE: Beauty should be quiet, gentle, and come from the heart.

HUSBANDS, HONOR YOUR WIVES

7 You husbands, in the same way, live with your wives according to knowledge, giving honor to the woman, as to the weaker vessel, as also being joint heirs of the grace of life, that your prayers may not be hindered.

BE OF ONE MIND

8 Finally, all of you be like-minded, compassionate, loving as brothers, tenderhearted, courteous,

DON'T RETALIATE

9 not rendering evil for evil, or insult for insult; but instead blessing, knowing that you were called to this, that you may inherit a blessing.

NOTE: Do not repay someone with evil or insults, but with a blessing.

HOLD YOUR TONGUE

10 For, "He who would love life and see good days, let him keep his tongue from evil and his lips from speaking deceit.

11 Let him turn away from evil and do good. Let him seek peace and pursue it."

NOTE: Enjoy life, avoid speaking evil and telling lies, and do good, for the Lord cares for those who do right, and his ears are open to their prayers.

GOD WILL REWARD YOU IF YOU SUFFER AND DO RIGHT

14 But even if you should suffer for righteousness' sake, you are blessed. "Don't fear what they fear, neither be troubled."

WORSHIP JESUS AND SHARE YOUR FAITH

15 But sanctify the Lord God in your hearts. Always be ready to give an answer to everyone who asks you a reason concerning the hope that is in you, with humility and fear,

NOTE: Believers should be ready to explain their hope in the Lord.

DO WHAT IS RIGHT

16 having a good conscience. Thus, while you are spoken against as evildoers, they may be disappointed who curse your good way of life in Christ.

NOTE: Follow Jesus, live a good life, and keep a clear conscience, and then those who speak evil against you will be shamed and embarrassed.

I PETER CHAPTER 4

SIN LOSES ITS POWER WHEN YOU SUFFER FOR JESUS

1 Therefore, since Christ suffered for us in the flesh, arm yourselves also with the same mind; for he who has suffered in the flesh has ceased from sin,

BE ANXIOUS TO DO THE WILL OF GOD

2 that you no longer should live the rest of your time in the flesh for the lusts of men, but for the will of God.

BE DISCIPLINED MEN OF PRAYER

7 But the end of all things is near. Therefore be of sound mind, self-controlled, and sober in prayer.

SHOW DEEP LOVE FOR EACH OTHER

8 And above all things be earnest in your love among yourselves, for love covers a multitude of sins.

SHARE YOUR HOME

9 Be hospitable to one another without grumbling.

NOTE: To grumble is to complain.

USE YOUR SPECIAL GIFTS

10 As each has received a gift, employ it in serving one another, as good managers of the grace of God in its various forms.

11 If anyone speaks, let it be as it were the very words of God. If anyone serves, let it be as of the strength which God supplies, that in all things God may be glorified through Jesus Christ, to whom belong the glory and the dominion forever and ever. Amen.

NOTE: Use the gifts God gives you.

BE GLAD IN SUFFERING FOR JESUS

12 Beloved, don't be astonished at the fiery trial which has come upon you to test you, as though a strange thing happened to you.

13 But because you are partakers of Christ's sufferings, rejoice, that at the revelation of his glory you also may rejoice with exceeding joy.

15 For let none of you suffer as a murderer, or a thief, or an evil doer, or a meddler in other men's matters.

16 But if one of you suffers for being a Christian, let him not be ashamed; but let him glorify God in this matter.

19 Therefore let them also who suffer according to the will of God in doing good entrust their souls to him, as to a faithful Creator.

NOTE: Endure suffering for Christ and you will be blessed with the great joy of seeing Jesus in his glory.

I PETER CHAPTER 5

FEED GOD'S FLOCK

2 Shepherd the flock of God which is among you, exercising the oversight, not under compulsion, but voluntarily, not for dishonest gain, but willingly;

LEAD BY EXAMPLE

3 not as lording it over those entrusted to you, but making yourselves examples to the flock.

NOTE: Elders should willingly watch over God's people through their own good example.

YOUNG MEN SHOULD ACCEPT ELDER AUTHORITY

5 Likewise, you younger ones, be subject to the elder. Yes, all of you clothe yourselves with humility, to subject yourselves to one another; for "God resists the proud, but gives grace to the humble."

BE HUMBLE

6 Humble yourselves therefore under the mighty hand of God, that he may exalt you in due time,

GIVE YOUR WORRIES TO GOD

7 casting all your worries on him, because he cares for you.

STAY ALERT TO THE DEVIL AND STAND FIRM

8 Be sober and self-controlled. Be watchful. Your adversary, the devil, walks around like a roaring lion, seeking whom he may devour.

9 Withstand him steadfast in your faith, knowing that your brothers who are in the world are undergoing the same sufferings.

GREET EACH OTHER WITH A KISS

14 Greet one another with a kiss of love. Peace be to all of you who are in Christ Jesus. Amen.

THE COMMANDS
OF 2 PETER

2 PETER

2 PETER CHAPTER 1

HAVE MORAL EXCELLENCE

5 Yes, and for this very cause adding on your part all diligence, in your faith supply moral excellence; and in moral excellence, knowledge;

HAVE SELF-CONTROL

6 and in knowledge, self-control; and in self-control perseverance; and in perseverance godliness;

SHARE BROTHERLY AFFECTION

7 and in godliness brotherly affection; and in brotherly affection, love.

8 For if these things are yours and abound, they make you to not be idle or unfruitful in the knowledge of our Lord Jesus Christ.

WORK HARD

10 Therefore, brothers, be more diligent to make your calling and election sure. For if you do these things, you will never stumble.

NOTE: Beyond salvation, a believer must work hard on those things God calls us to do, and we will be welcomed into God's eternal Kingdom.

2 PETER CHAPTER 3

REMEMBER THE COMMANDS OF JESUS

2 that you should remember the words which were spoken before by the holy prophets and the commandment of us, the apostles of the Lord and Savior:

BE PATIENT; A DAY IS LIKE A THOUSAND YEARS TO THE LORD

8 But don't forget this one thing, beloved, that one day is with the Lord as a thousand years, and a thousand years as one day.

LIVE A PEACEFUL LIFE

14 Therefore, beloved, seeing that you look for these things, be diligent to be found in peace, without defect and blameless in his sight.

DON'T BE FOOLED BY WICKED PEOPLE

17 You therefore, beloved, knowing these things beforehand, beware, lest being carried away with the error of the wicked, you fall from your own steadfastness.

GROW IN SPIRITUAL KNOWLEDGE

18 But grow in the grace and knowledge of our Lord and Savior Jesus Christ. To him be the glory both now and forever. Amen.

THE COMMANDS OF 1 JOHN

1 JOHN

1 JOHN CHAPTER 2

DON'T LOVE THIS EVIL WORLD

15 Don't love the world or the things that are in the world. If anyone loves the world, the Father's love isn't in him.

STAY FAITHFUL TO TEACHING

24 Therefore, as for you, let that remain in you which you heard from the beginning. If that which you heard from the beginning remains in you, you also will remain in the Son, and in the Father.

REMAIN IN FELLOWSHIP WITH JESUS

28 Now, little children, remain in him, that when he appears, we may have boldness, and not be ashamed before him at his coming.

1 JOHN CHAPTER 3

DO WHAT IS RIGHT

7 Little children, let no one lead you astray. He who does righteousness is righteous, even as he is righteous.

STAY THE COURSE IF THE WORLD HATES YOU

13 Don't be surprised, my brothers, if the world hates you.

SHOW COMPASSION

17 But whoever has the world's goods and sees his brother in need, then closes his heart of compassion against him, how does God's love remain in him?

NOTE: Help those less fortunate.

LOVE EACH OTHER

18 My little children, let's not love in word only, or with the tongue only, but in deed and truth.

NOTE: Love is more than words, but action.

BELIEVE IN JESUS AND LOVE ONE ANOTHER

23 This is his commandment, that we should believe in the name of his Son, Jesus Christ, and love one another, even as he commanded.

1 JOHN CHAPTER 4

STAY AWAY FROM FALSE PROPHETS

1 Beloved, don't believe every spirit, but test the spirits, whether they are of God, because many false prophets have gone out into the world.

BE LOVING AND KIND

7 Beloved, let's love one another, for love is of God; and everyone who loves has been born of God, and knows God.

11 Beloved, if God loved us in this way, we also ought to love one another.

THOSE WHO LOVE GOD MUST LOVE OTHER BELIEVERS

21 This commandment we have from him, that he who loves God should also love his brother.

NOTE: A believer who loves God but hates his brother is a liar.

1 JOHN CHAPTER 5

PRAY FOR SINNERS

16 If anyone sees his brother sinning a sin not leading to death, he shall ask, and God will give him life for those who sin not leading to death.

There is a sin leading to death. I don't say that he should make a request concerning this.

NOTE: Pray for those who sin, but know God is their final judge.

STAY AWAY FROM ANYTHING THAT REPLACES GOD

21 Little children, keep yourselves from idols.

THE COMMANDS
OF 2 JOHN

2 JOHN

2 JOHN CHAPTER 1

LOVE ONE ANOTHER

5 Now I beg you, dear lady, not as though I wrote to you a new commandment, but that which we had from the beginning, that we love one another.

LOVE IS DOING WHAT GOD COMMANDED US TO DO

6 This is love, that we should walk according to his commandments. This is the commandment, even as you heard from the beginning, that you should walk in it.

NOTE: One of the most important things to do in life is love one another.

BEWARE OF FALSE TEACHERS

8 Watch yourselves, that we don't lose the things which we have accomplished, but that we receive a full reward.

10 If anyone comes to you, and doesn't bring this teaching, don't receive him into your house, and don't welcome him,

11 for he who welcomes him participates in his evil deeds.

THE COMMANDS
OF 3 JOHN

3 JOHN

3 JOHN CHAPTER 1

SUPPORT TEACHERS AND MISSIONARIES

8 We therefore ought to receive such, that we may be fellow workers for the truth.

FOLLOW WHAT IS GOOD

11 Beloved, don't imitate that which is evil, but that which is good. He who does good is of God. He who does evil hasn't seen God.

THE COMMANDS OF JUDE

JUDE

JUDE CHAPTER 1

DEFEND THE FAITH AND TRUTH

3 Beloved, while I was very eager to write to you about our common salvation, I was constrained to write to you exhorting you to contend earnestly for the faith which was once for all delivered to the saints.

REMEMBER THE APOSTLE'S PREDICTIONS

17 But you, beloved, remember the words which have been spoken before by the apostles of our Lord Jesus Christ.

18 They said to you, "In the last time there will be mockers, walking after their own ungodly lusts."

NOTE: Stay away from mockers of God who stir up division.

BUILD EACH OTHER UP IN FAITH

20 But you, beloved, keep building up yourselves on your most holy faith, praying in the Holy Spirit.

AWAIT THE MERCY OF JESUS

21 Keep yourselves in God's love, looking for the mercy of our Lord Jesus Christ to eternal life.

SHOW MERCY TO THOSE WITH WAVERING FAITH

22 On some have compassion, making a distinction,

NOTE: Be kind to those struggling with their faith.

BE MERCIFUL TO SINNERS WHILE HATING SIN

23 and some save, snatching them out of the fire with fear, hating even the clothing stained by the flesh.

NOTE: While you love those who struggle, hate the sin they commit.

THE COMMANDS OF REVELATION

REVELATION

REVELATION CHAPTER 2

REPENT AND DO THE WORKS YOU DID BEFORE

5 Remember therefore from where you have fallen, and repent and do the first works; or else I am coming to you swiftly, and will move your lamp stand out of its place, unless you repent.

BE VICTORIOUS AND BE GIVEN FRUIT FROM THE TREE OF LIFE

7 He who has an ear, let him hear what the Spirit says to the assemblies. To him who overcomes I will give to eat from the tree of life, which is in the Paradise of my God.

NOTE: Those who endure to the end are given eternal life.

REMAIN FAITHFUL AND RECEIVE THE CROWN

10 Don't be afraid of the things which you are about to suffer. Behold, the devil is about to throw some of you into prison, that you may be tested; and you will have oppression for ten days. Be faithful to death, and I will give you the crown of life.

NOTE: Withstand the tests of the devil and receive eternal life.

BE VICTORIOUS AND AVOID THE SECOND DEATH

11 He who has an ear, let him hear what the Spirit says to the assemblies. He who overcomes won't be harmed by the second death.

REPENT OF YOUR SIN

16 Repent therefore, or else I am coming to you quickly, and I will make war against them with the sword of my mouth.

BE VICTORIOUS AND RECEIVE MANNA AND A NEW NAME

17 He who has an ear, let him hear what the Spirit says to the assemblies. To him who overcomes, to him I will give of the hidden manna, and I will give him a white stone, and on the stone a new name written, which no one knows but he who receives it.

NOTE: Manna is spiritual nourishment.

HOLD TIGHTLY TO WHAT YOU HAVE

25 Nevertheless, hold that which you have firmly until I come.

LISTEN TO THE SPIRIT

29 He who has an ear, let him hear what the Spirit says to the assemblies.

REVELATION CHAPTER 3

STRENGTHEN YOUR ACTIONS AND DEEDS

2 Wake up and keep the things that remain, which you were about to throw away, for I have found no works of yours perfected before my God.

REPENT OR BE PUNISHED

3 Remember therefore how you have received and heard. Keep it and repent. If therefore you won't watch, I will come as a thief, and you won't know what hour I will come upon you.

NOTE: If you do not meet God's requirements, repent and return to God.

LISTEN TO THE SPIRIT

6 He who has an ear, let him hear what the Spirit says to the assemblies.

HOLD ON SO NO ONE CAN TAKE YOUR CROWN

11. I am coming quickly! Hold firmly that which you have, so that no one takes your crown.

13 He who has an ear, let him hear what the Spirit says to the assemblies.

TURN FROM INDIFFERENCE AND BECOME ENTHUSIASTIC

19 As many as I love, I reprove and chasten. Be zealous therefore, and repent.

NOTE: God disciplines those who are indifferent to him.

22 He who has an ear, let him hear what the Spirit says to the assemblies."

REVELATION CHAPTER 13

SOLVE THE PUZZLE OF THE BEAST

18 Here is wisdom. He who has understanding, let him calculate the number of the beast, for it is the number of a man. His number is six hundred sixty-six.

NOTE: The beast and the number 666 represent complete evil.

REVELATION CHAPTER 14

WORSHIP GOD

7 He said with a loud voice, "Fear the Lord, and give him glory; for the hour of his judgment has come. Worship him who made the heaven, the earth, the sea, and the springs of waters!"

NOTE: Worship God at all times and everything he does.

REVELATION CHAPTER 22

HARMFUL OR VILE, RIGHTEOUS OR HOLY, LET IT CONTINUE

11 He who acts unjustly, let him act unjustly still. He who is filthy, let him be filthy still. He

who is righteous, let him do righteousness still. He who is holy, let him be holy still."

COME AND DRINK FROM THE WATER OF LIFE

17 The Spirit and the bride say, "Come!" He who hears, let him say, "Come!" He who is thirsty, let him come. He who desires, let him take the water of life freely.

SECTION THREE

CHARACTERISTICS OF NEW TESTAMENT BELIEVERS

CHARACTERISTICS OF A NEW TESTAMENT BELIEVER

BELIEFS

1. Put On the Shining Armor of Right Living (Romans)
2. Accept Different Christian Beliefs (Romans)
3. Stay Away From the Lazy Believers (2 Thessalonians)

BUSINESS/WORK/DISCIPLINE

1. Work Hard to Enter God's Kingdom (Luke)
2. Working On the Sabbath (John)
3. Work Hard (Romans)
4. Use Your God-Given Gifts (Romans)

5. Work Enthusiastically for the Lord (I Corinthians)
6. Do God's Work (I Corinthians)
7. Avoid Distractions (I Corinthians)
8. Do Your Very Best at your Work (Galatians)
9. You Reap What You Sow (Galatians)
10. Work Hard (Philippians)
11. Work Hard (Colossians)
12. Be Task Focused (1 Timothy)
13. Work Hard (2 Timothy)
14. Farmers Enjoy First Fruit (2 Timothy)
15. Work Hard (2 Peter)

BODY

1. Give Your Bodies to God (Romans)
2. Circumcision (I Corinthians)
3. Circumcision (Philippians)

CHARACTER POSITIVES

1. Strive to be Perfect (Matt)
2. Be Like Children (Mark)

3. Keep Seeking (Luke)
4. Don't Be Afraid (Luke)
5. Be Humble (Luke)
6. Keep Asking (Luke)
7. Be Like Children (Luke)
8. Be Patient (Romans)
9. Greet Each Other (Romans)
10. Stand Firm (I Corinthians)
11. Run to Win (I Corinthians)
12. Only Boast of the Lord (2 Corinthians)
13. Do What is Right and Good (Galatians)
14. Be Humble (Philippians)
15. Be Full of Joy (Philippians)
16. Be Unselfish (Philippians)
17. Don't Worry (Philippians)
18. Be Kind (Colossians)
19. Forgive (Colossians)
20. Stay Alert (1 Thessalonians)
21. Be Joyful (1 Thessalonians)
22. Greet with a Kiss (1 Thessalonians)

23. Be Thankful (1 Thessalonians)
24. Be Gentle and Be Kind (2 Timothy)
25. Be Strong and Bold (2 Timothy)
26. Be Strong with Grace (2 Timothy)
27. Be Patient (James)
28. Use Self-Control (1 Peter)
29. Be Obedient (1 Peter)
30. Be Humble (1 Peter)
31. Focus on the Beauty Within (1 Peter)

CHARACTER LIFESTYLE

1. A Tree Identifies the Fruit (Matt)
2. Live Decent Lives (Romans)
3. Live in the Light (Ephesians)
4. Live Like Jesus (Philippians)
5. Be a Mature Christian (Philippians)
6. Live a Quiet Life (1 Thessalonians)
7. Watch How You Live (1 Timothy)
8. Fight Well in the Lord's Battles (1 Timothy)
9. Be an Example (1 Timothy)

10. Be an Example for Others (Titus)
11. Follow the Straight Path (Hebrews)
12. Behave Well Around Unbelievers (1 Peter)
13. Be Holy (1 Peter)
14. Do What is Right (1 Peter)
15. Use your Special Gifts (1 Peter)
16. Lead by Example (1 Peter)
17. Live A Peaceful Life (2 Peter)
18. Have Moral Excellence (2 Peter)
19. Have Self Control (2 Peter)
20. Stay the Course if the World Hates You (1 John)
21. Turn from Indifference and Become Enthusiastic (Revelation)

CHARACTER NEGATIVES

1. Don't Be a Hypocrite (Luke)
2. Do Not Brag (Romans)
3. Don't Boast (I Corinthians)
4. Be Free from Pride and Fear (I Corinthians)

5. Avoid Being Conceited or Jealous (Galatians)
6. Stop Lying (Ephesians)
7. Don't Let Anger Control You (Ephesians)
8. Stop Stealing (Ephesians)
9. Don't Use Abusive Language (Ephesians)
10. No Drunkenness (Ephesians)
11. Don't Argue (Philippians)
12. Get Rid of Anger (Colossians)
13. Don't Lie (Colossians)
14. Avoid Jealousy and Selfishness (James)
15. Don't Favor Some People Over Others (James)
16. Get Rid of Hatred (1 Peter)

CHILDREN

1. Honor your Mother and Father (Matt)
2. Obey your Parents (Ephesians)
3. Raise Children with Loving Discipline (Ephesians)
4. Children Obey (Colossians)
5. Use Fair Discipline (Colossians)

COMMUNICATION/SPEECH/GREETINGS

1. God Will Answer Through You (Luke)
2. Greet Each Other (Romans)
3. Speaking in Tongues (I Corinthians)
4. Speaking in Prophesy (I Corinthians)
5. Tongues Require Interpretation (I Corinthians)
6. Listen (2 Corinthians)
7. Don't Use Abusive Language (Ephesians)
8. Avoid Foolish Talk (Ephesians)
9. Don't Argue (Philippians)
10. Conversation Should Be Gracious (Colossians)
11. Read This Letter (1 Thessalonians)
12. Don't Waste Time in Meaningless Discussion (1 Timothy)
13. Don't Waste Time Arguing (1 Timothy)
14. Avoid Foolish Discussions (1 Timothy)
15. Stop Fighting Over Words (2 Timothy)
16. Avoid Foolish Talk (2 Timothy)

17. Run from Arguments (2 Timothy)
18. Avoid Slander (Titus)
19. Avoid Quarrels Over Theological Ideas (Titus)
20. Be Quick to Listen, Slow to Speak, Slow to Anger (James)
21. Watch What You Say and Do (James)
22. Avoid Blessing and Curses from the Same Mouth (James)
23. Do Not Swear or Take an Oath (James)
24. Hold your Tongue (1 Peter)
25. Greet Each Other with a Kiss (1 Peter)

COVENANT

1. Remember the Body and Blood of Jesus (Mark)
2. Partake in My Body (I Corinthians)
3. Partake in My Blood (I Corinthians)

DISCIPLESHIP

1. Discipleship Guidelines (Matt)

2. Plant Seeds (Matt)
3. Discipleship (Mark)
4. Plant Seeds (Mark)
5. Go into the World and Preach the Gospel (Mark)
6. Fish for Men's Souls (Luke)
7. Plant Seeds (Luke)
8. Discipleship Travel (Luke)
9. The Harvest is Great (Luke)
10. Human Souls Are Ready for Harvesting (John)
11. Be A Disciple (John)
12. Feed His Sheep (John)
13. Preach Everywhere (Acts)
14. Feed God's People (Acts)
15. Share the Good News (Colossians)
16. Carry Out the Ministry (Colossians)
17. Preach the Good News (2 Timothy)
18. Preach the Word, In Season or Not (2 Timothy)
19. Carry Out the Ministry (2 Timothy)

20. Feed God's Flock (1 Peter)
21. Share Your Faith (1 Peter)

ENEMIES

1. Settle Your Differences (Matt)
2. Do Not Resist Those Who Hurt You (Matt)
3. Love Your Enemies (Matt)
4. Love your Enemies (Luke)
5. Bless the Persecutor (Romans)
6. Avoid Divisions (Romans)
7. Don't Be Intimidated by Enemies (Philippians)

ELDER/PASTOR REQUIREMENTS

1. Elder/Pastor Requirements (1 Timothy)
2. Take Care of Widows (1 Timothy)
3. Widows as Church Workers (1 Timothy)
4. Elders Should Be Paid Well (1 Timothy)
5. Elder Discipline (1 Timothy)
6. Elder Requirements (2 Timothy)

EVIL

1. Cast Out Evil (I Corinthians)
2. Plan No Evil (I Corinthians)
3. Avoid Bad Company (I Corinthians)
4. Don't Team with Wickedness (2 Corinthians)
5. Stay Away from Evil (1 Thessalonians)
6. Don't Repay Evil (1 Thessalonians)
7. Run from Evil (1 Timothy)
8. Turn from Evil (2 Timothy)
9. Get Rid of All Evil (James)
10. Resist the Devil, and He Will Flee (James)
11. Stay Alert to the Devil and Stand Firm (1 Peter)
12. Don't Love this Evil World (1 John)
13. Solve the Puzzle of the Beast (Revelation)

FAITH

1. Measure Yourself by Faith (Romans)
2. Pass the Test of Genuine Faith (2 Corinthians)

3. Cling Tightly to your Faith (1 Timothy)
4. It's Impossible to Please God Without Faith (Hebrews)
5. Share your Faith (1 Peter)
6. Build Each Other Up in Faith (Jude)

FOOD/DRINK/WATER

1. Don't Worry about Clothes, Food, or Drink (Matt)
2. Abstain from Food offered to Idols (Acts)
3. If God Calls it Clean, Don't Call it Impure (Acts)
4. Eating Guidelines (Romans)
5. Eating Conscience (I Corinthians)
6. Food Offered to Idols (I Corinthians)
7. Wine for Medicine (1 Timothy)
8. Fast in Private (Matt)

FORGIVENESS

1. Forgive (Mark)
2. Don't Repay Evil (1 Thessalonians)

GIFTS
1. Desire Godly Gifts (I Corinthians)
2. Ask for Special Abilities (I Corinthians)
3. Be Thankful (1 Thessalonians)
4. Use your Spiritual Gifts (1 Timothy)

GOD
1. Love God with All your Heart (Mark)
2. Serve God (Luke)
3. Love your God with All your Heart (Luke)
4. Trust in God (John)
5. Do All For God (I Corinthians)
6. Don't Test God (I Corinthians)
7. Do God's Work (I Corinthians)
8. Sing Songs to God (Ephesians)
9. Give Thanks to God (Ephesians)
10. Follow God in Everything (Ephesians)
11. Put on God's Armor (Ephesians)
12. Sing to God (Colossians)
13. Remember, God Provides Rest (2 Thessalonians)

14. Don't Turn from God (Hebrews)
15. Follow God's Examples (Hebrews)
16. Fully Trust God (Hebrews)
17. Run your Race for God (Hebrews)
18. Be a Sacrifice for God (Hebrews)
19. Come Closer to God, and He Comes Closer to You (James)
20. Be Anxious to Do the Will of God (1 Peter)
21. Worship God (Revelation)

GOOD DEEDS

1. Do your Good Deeds in Private (Matt)
2. Let Your Good Deeds Shine (Matt)
3. Do What is Right and Good (Galatians)
4. Be Devoted to Good Deeds (Titus)
5. Live Honorably and Do Good Works (James)
6. Do What is Right (1 Peter)
7. Do What is Right (1 John)
8. Do the Works You Did Before (Revelation)

9. Strengthen your Actions and Deeds (Revelation)

HEAVEN FOCUSED

1. Store your Treasures in Heaven (Matt)
2. Live As a Citizen of Heaven (Philippians)
3. Focus on Heaven (Colossians)
4. Follow the Straight Path (Hebrews)
5. Focus On Entering the Place of Rest (Hebrews)
6. Be Victorious and Be Given Fruit from the Tree of Life (Revelation)
7. Remain Faithful and Receive the Crown (Revelation)
8. Come and Drink the Water of Life (Revelation)
9. Be Victorious and Avoid the Second Death (Revelation)
10. Be Victorious and Receive Manna and a New Name (Revelation)
11. Hold On So No One Can Take Your Crown (Revelation)

HOLY SPIRIT

1. Receive the Holy Spirit (John)
2. Don't Smother the Holy Spirit (1 Thessalonians)

HUSBANDS/WIVES/MEN/WOMEN

1. Marriage and Divorce (I Corinthians)
2. Marriage and Sex (I Corinthians)
3. Unmarried Benefits (I Corinthians)
4. Head Coverings (I Corinthians)
5. Submit to One Another (Ephesians)
6. Avoid Immorality (Ephesians)
7. Wives Submit (Colossians)
8. Husbands Submit (Colossians)
9. Women Dress Appropriately (1 Timothy)
10. Older Men Requirements (Titus)
11. Older Women Requirements (Titus)
12. Younger Women Requirements (Titus)
13. Younger Men Requirements (Titus)
14. Wives Accept Your Husband's Plans (1 Peter)

15. Husbands, Honor your Wives (1 Peter)
16. Young Men Should Accept Elder Authority (1 Peter)

IDOLATRY

1. Avoid Idolatry (I Corinthians)

ILLNESS

1. Anoint the Sick with Oil and Pray (James)

JESUS FOCUSED

1. Obey God, follow Jesus (Matt)
2. Follow Jesus (Matt)
3. Jesus Gives Rest (Matt)
4. Take Up your Cross and Follow Jesus (Matt)
5. Follow Jesus (Mark)
6. Listen to Jesus (Mark)
7. Take Up your Cross and Follow Jesus (Mark)
8. Sell Your Possessions, Give to the Poor and Follow Jesus (Mark)

9. Follow Jesus (Luke)
10. Follow Jesus, Don't Look Back (Luke)
11. Remember His Body and Blood (Luke)
12. Follow Jesus (John)
13. Trust in Jesus (John)
14. As for You, Follow Jesus (John)
15. Live in Jesus (John)
16. Be Glad in the Lord (Philippians)
17. Stay True to the Lord (Philippians)
18. Live Like Jesus (Philippians)
19. Follow Jesus (Colossians)
20. Represent Jesus (Colossians)
21. Never Be Ashamed of the Lord (2 Timothy)
22. Keep your Trust in the Lord (Hebrews)
23. Keep your Eyes on Jesus (Hebrews)
24. Seek What the Lord Wants (James)
25. Worship Jesus and Share your Faith (1 Peter)
26. Remain in Fellowship with Jesus (1 John)
27. Believe in Jesus (1 John)
28. Await the Mercy of Jesus (Jude)

JUDGING

1. Who To Judge (I Corinthians)
2. Don't Judge (I Corinthians)
3. Don't Criticize and Judge Others (James)
4. You Are Judged On What You Do (1 Peter)
5. Respect Everyone (1 Peter)

JUSTICE/FIGHTING

1. Show Mercy (Luke)
2. Settle your Differences Before Going to Court (Luke)
3. Handing Legal Disputes (1 Corinthians)
4. Use Fair Discipline (Colossians)
5. Obey the Government (Titus)
6. Accept the Lord's Discipline (Hebrews)
7. Don't Favor Some People Over Others (James)
8. Submit to Authority (1 Peter)
9. Don't Retaliate (1 Peter)

LAWS AND COMMANDMENTS/BIBLE

1. Jesus came to Fulfill the Law and Commandments (Matt)
2. Remember the Ten Commandments (Mark)
3. Remember the Commandments (Luke)
4. Obey the Authorities and Laws (Romans)
5. Remember your Past (Ephesians)
6. Hold Firmly to the Word (Philippians)
7. Avoid Human Thinking (Colossians)
8. Don't Scoff at Prophecies (1 Thessalonians)
9. Stand Firm to the Truth (2 Thessalonians)
10. Women Don't Teach Men (1 Timothy)
11. Read Scripture to the Church (1 Timothy)
12. Wholesome Teaching Promotes a Godly Life (1 Timothy)
13. Be Wary of Godless Teaching (1 Timothy)
14. Obey Commands without Wavering (1 Timothy)

15. Hold Onto Truthful Teaching (2 Timothy)
16. Guard the Truth (2 Timothy)
17. Teach Great Truths (2 Timothy)
18. Gently Instruct Those Who Oppose the Truth (2 Timothy)
19. Stay Away from Scoffers (2 Timothy)
20. Remain Faithful to the Teaching (2 Timothy)
21. Listen and Obey (Hebrews)
22. Church Teachers Are Judged Strictly (James)
23. Remember the Commands of Jesus (2 Peter)
24. Love is Doing What God Commanded Us to Do (2 John)
25. Support Teachers and Missionaries (3 John)
26. Remember the Apostle's Predictions (Jude)
27. Listen to the Spirit (Revelation)
28. Harmful or Vile, Righteous or Holy, Let it Continue (Revelation)

LOVE/JOY/PEACE

1. Love Others (Mark)
2. Love Each Other (John)
3. Love People (Romans)
4. How to Treat Other's (Romans)
5. Love Your Neighbor (Romans)
6. Accept Others (Romans)
7. Show Kindness and Love (I Corinthians)
8. Live in Harmony (I Corinthians)
9. Make Love Your Highest Goal (I Corinthians)
10. Love (Colossians)
11. Live in Peace (Colossians)
12. Be Filled with Love (1 Timothy)
13. Motivate Others to Love and Kindness (Hebrews)
14. Love Each Other (Hebrews)
15. Show Deep Love for Each Other (1 Peter)
16. Share Brotherly Affection (2 Peter)
17. Show Compassion (1 John)

18. Love Each Other (1 John)
19. Love One Another (1 John)
20. Be Loving and Kind (1 John)
21. Those Who Love God Must Love other Believers (1 John)
22. Love One Another (2 John)
23. Love is Doing What God Commanded Us to Do (2 John)

MATERIAL POSSESSIONS
1. Don't Worry about Food and Clothes (Luke)
2. Sell Your Possessions (Luke)
3. Be Content with Food and Clothing (1 Timothy)
4. Avoid Worldly Desires (1 Peter)

MONEY
1. Give to God and Give to the Government (Matt)
2. Don't Extort Money (Luke)

3. Guard Against Greed (Luke)
4. Give to Caesar, Give to God (Luke)
5. The Father's House is not a Marketplace (John)
6. Money Collection-Tithing (I Corinthians)
7. Give What You Can (2 Corinthians)
8. Be a Cheerful Giver (2 Corinthians)
9. Pay Those Who Teach You the Word (Galatians)
10. Money is the Root of All Evil (1 Timothy)
11. Trust in God, not Money (1 Timothy)
12. Don't Love Money (Hebrews)
13. God Humbles the Rich (James)
14. The Rich Will Weep and Groan (James)
15. Avoid Worldly Desires (1 Peter)

NEIGHBORS/PEOPLE

1. Do not Judge (Matt)
2. Do unto Others (Matt)
3. Show Mercy (Matt)
4. Give to Others (Matt)

5. Strengthen Each Other (I Corinthians)
6. Love your Neighbor (Galatians)
7. Share Each Other's Troubles and Problems (Galatians)
8. Encourage Each Other (Philippians)
9. Encourage Each Other (1 Thessalonians)
10. Encourage the Lazy, Frightened, and Weak (1 Thessalonians)
11. Show No Favoritism (1 Timothy)
12. Treat Older Men Well (1 Timothy)
13. Treat Older Women Well (1 Timothy)
14. Help With the Urgent Needs of Others (Titus)
15. Don't Favor Some People Over Others (James)
16. Divided Loyalty Leads to Sorrow (James)
17. Share your Home (1 Peter)
18. Respect Everyone (1 Peter)
19. Show Mercy to Those with Wavering Faith (Jude)

THE POOR

1. Give to the Poor (Mark)
2. Sell Your Possessions, Give to the Poor, and Follow Jesus (Mark)
3. Give to the Poor (Luke)
4. Give to the Poor (Luke)
5. Invite the Poor (Luke)
6. Use Worldly Resources to Benefit Others (Luke)
7. God Honors the Poor (James)
8. Remember, The Poor Inherit the Kingdom Of God (James)

PRAYING

1. Follow this Example of Prayer (Matt)
2. Pray in Private (Matt)
3. Believe and Receive (Matt)
4. How You Should Pray (Luke)
5. Ask and You Will Receive (John)
6. Pray (Colossians)
7. Always Pray (1 Thessalonians)

8. Pray for the Lord's Message (2 Thessalonians)
9. Pray for the People (1 Timothy)
10. Pray with Hands Lifted (1 Timothy)
11. Pray for Spiritual Leaders (Hebrews)
12. Pray During Hardships (James)
13. Be Disciplined Men of Prayer (1 Peter)
14. Give your Worries to God (1 Peter)
15. Pray for Sinners (1 John)

SALVATION

1. Work Hard to Enter God's Kingdom (Luke)
2. You Must Be Born Again (John)
3. Seek Eternal Life, Not Food (John)
4. Receive the Holy Spirit (John)
5. Trust in the Light (John)
6. Be Baptized (Acts)
7. Be A New Person (Romans)
8. Open your Heart to Salvation (2 Corinthians)
9. Cleanse Yourself (2 Corinthians)

10. Become a New Person (Ephesians)
11. Live in the Light (Ephesians)
12. Live As a Citizen of Heaven (Philippians)
13. Fight the Good Fight for Eternal Life (1 Timothy)
14. Hold Onto Salvation (Hebrews)
15. Remember God Paid a Price to Save You (1 Peter)
16. Be Victorious and Avoid the Second Death (Revelation)

SECOND COMING

1. No One Knows When Jesus Will Return (Mark)
2. Keep Watch (Mark)
3. Wait for his Return (Luke)
4. Work Hard to Enter God's Kingdom (Luke)
5. Keep Watch for the Return of Jesus (Luke)
6. Keep Watch for the Return of Jesus (Luke)
7. The Kingdom of God is Near (Luke)
8. Stay Alert (1 Thessalonians)

9. Don't Be Fooled By the Day of the Lord's Arrival (2 Thessalonians)
10. Be Patient and Wait for the Lord's Return (James)
11. Be Patient; A Day is Like a Thousand Years to the Lord (2 Peter)

SERVANTS/GENEROSITY

1. Give to Others (Matt)
2. Be a Servant to Everyone (Mark)
3. The Greatest People Are Servants (Luke)
4. Wash Each Other's Feet (John)
5. Help Others (Romans)
6. Help God's Children (Romans)
7. Think of Others (I Corinthians)
8. Help With the Urgent Needs of Others (Titus)
9. Share your Home (1 Peter)

SEX

1. Abstain from Sexual Immorality (Acts)

2. Avoid Sexual Immorality (I Corinthians)
3. Avoid Immorality (Ephesians)
4. Avoid Sexual Sin (1 Thessalonians)
5. Run from Lust and Evil Thoughts (2 Timothy)

SINS/REPENTING

1. Turn from your Sins (Matt)
2. Avoid Sins and Vows (Matt)
3. Repent of your Sins (Mark)
4. Don't Tolerate Sin in Yourself (Mark)
5. Prove that you have Repented (Luke)
6. Rebuke Sin (Luke)
7. Stop Sinning (John)
8. Repent of your Sins and Be Baptized (Acts)
9. Repent of your Sins (Acts)
10. Repent of Wickedness (Acts)
11. Don't Serve Sin (Romans)
12. Run From Sin (1 Corinthians)
13. Stop Sinning (1 Corinthians)
14. Stop Sinning (Ephesians)

15. Don't Excuse Sins (Ephesians)
16. Avoid Immorality (Ephesians)
17. Deaden Yourself to Sin (Colossians)
18. Strip Off Sin (Hebrews)
19. God Never Tempts You to Do Wrong (James)
20. Confess your Sins to Each Other (James)
21. Cleanse your Sins by Obeying the Truth (1 Peter)
22. Sin Loses its Power When You Suffer for Jesus Peter)
23. Be Merciful to Sinners While Hating Sin (Jude)
24. Repent (Revelation)
25. Repent of Your Sin (Revelation)
26. Repent of your Sin (Revelation)
27. Repent or Be Punished (Revelation)

SUFFERING/TROUBLES

1. Be Glad when You Are Persecuted (Matt)
2. Endure All Trials and be Saved (Mark)

3. Slaves Don't Worry (1 Corinthians)
4. Slaves and Slave Owners (Ephesians)
5. Slaves Obey (Colossians)
6. Slave Owners (Colossians)
7. Slaves Show Full Respect (1 Timothy)
8. Endure Suffering (2 Timothy)
9. Slave Requirements (Titus)
10. Consider Troubles a Joy (James)
11. Pray During Hardships (James)
12. Slaves Submit to Masters (1 Peter)
13. Be Glad in Suffering for Jesus (1 Peter)
14. God Will Reward You if You Suffer and Do Right (1 Peter)

TEACHING/LEARNING (Correct)

1. Open your Hearts to the Truth (2 Corinthians)
2. Grow As a Christian (2 Corinthians)
3. Guide Believers Back to the Path (Galatians)
4. Let the Holy Spirit Guide your Life (Galatians)

5. Avoid Human Thinking (Colossians)
6. Test Everything (1 Thessalonians)
7. Be a Mature Christian (Philippians)
8. Focus On What is True and Pure (Philippians)
9. Wholesome Teaching Promotes a Godly Life (1 Timothy)
10. Remain Faithful to the Teaching (2 Timothy)
11. Teach Great Truths (2 Timothy)
12. Silence Those Who Refuse to Obey (Titus)
13. Promote Right Living (Titus)
14. Warn Divisive People (Titus)
15. Become Mature in Understanding (Hebrews)
16. Meet Together (Hebrews)
17. Avoid Strange Ideas (Hebrews)
18. Listen and Obey (Hebrews)
19. Follow the Example of Those Who Teach the Word (Hebrews)
20. Obey Spiritual Leaders and Pray for Them (Hebrews)

21. Church Teachers Are Judged Strictly (James)
22. Crave Pure Spiritual Milk (1 Peter)
23. Be of One Mind (1 Peter)
24. Grow in Spiritual Knowledge (2 Peter)
25. Stay Faithful to Teaching (1 John)
26. Support Teachers and Missionaries (3 John)
27. Follow What Is Good (3 John)
28. Show Mercy to Those with Wavering Faith (Jude)
29. Defend the Faith and Truth (Jude)
30. Hold Tightly to What You Have (Revelation)
31. Listen to the Spirit (Revelation)

TEACHING (False, Mockers, Scoffers)

1. Don't Be Mislead by False Things (Mark)
2. Beware of Pharisees (Luke)
3. Beware Teachers of the Law (Luke)
4. Don't Mock the Truth (Acts)
5. Put Away Idols (Acts)

6. Beware of False Teachers (Acts)
7. Women Silent in the Church (I Corinthians)
8. Stay Away from Scoffers (2 Timothy)
9. Don't Be Fooled by Wicked People (2 Peter)
10. Stay Away from False Prophets (1 John)
11. Stay Away from Anything that Replaces God (1 John)
12. Beware of False Teachers (2 John)

WISDOM

1. Understand True Wisdom-Become a Fool (I Corinthians)
2. Be Wise (Colossians)
3. Seek Wisdom (James)

SECTION FOUR

CONDENSED CHARACTER TRAITS OF THE NEW TESTAMENT CHRISTIAN

BELIEFS

The believer is dedicated to living right based on the word of God and accepting differences in beliefs but stays away from lazy believers.

BUSINESS/WORK

The Christian believer is hardworking and task-focused, uses God-given gifts, and enthusiastically works for God.

BODY

A believer must give his body to God. In viewing God's mercy, offer your bodies as a living sacrifice, holy and pleasing to God—this is true and proper worship.

CHARACTER TRAITS

Christians should be humble and patient, unselfish, joyful, thankful, gentle and kind, and never afraid. They strive to be perfect, only boast of the Lord, and focus on doing what is right and good.

CHARACTER LIVING

A believer lives in the light and tries to live a quiet, peaceful, holy, and mature life while trying to live as Jesus did. They focus on staying the course even when the world hates them, maintaining self-control, and behaving well with unbelievers. They also focus on doing right.

CHARACTER NEGATIVES

Some of the main things Christians should avoid are anger, hatred, lying, stealing, bragging, drunkenness, arguing, jealousy, selfishness, and being a hypocrite.

CHILDREN

Children should always obey their parents and be raised with love and discipline.

COMMUNICATION/SPEECH

It is essential to listen and be gracious in your speech; God will give you the words to respond. You should not argue, fight, swear, use abusive language, or get caught up in foolish or meaningless discussions, and you should always watch what you say and do.

COVENANT

A believer should always remember the body and blood of Jesus. A covenant is an agreement where God makes promises to his people and where God requires certain conduct from them.

DISCIPLESHIP

A believer should plant the seeds of the gospel, fish for men's souls by preaching the good news, in season or out, and continually feed God's flock by sharing their faith.

ENEMIES

Believers are to love and bless their enemies but not be intimated by them and to settle differences, if possible, to avoid divisions.

ELDER/PASTOR REQUIREMENTS

They should be paid well, and the Bible lists specific requirements for being an Elder or Pastor, which are found in 1 Timothy.

EVIL

Believers are to avoid, run, and turn from evil, cast out evil, not team with evil or wickedness, and not love this evil world.

FAITH

Christians are measured by faith and must cling tightly to it and build each other up in faith. Believers must pass the test of genuine faith, and it is impossible to please God without faith.

FOOD

Believers should not worry about food or drink but abstain from food offered to idols. Wine can be used for medicine, and fasting should be done privately. Most food is considered clean in the New Testament.

FORGIVENESS

Believers are to forgive and not repay evil. Forgiveness means to let go of anger, bitterness, slander, malice, and wrath and instead be kind to one another, and to become tenderhearted and forgiving with each other, as God in Christ forgave you.

GIFTS

Christians are to desire special gifts and abilities, be thankful for them, and use them.

GOD

We are to do all for God. Serve him, thank him, love him, trust him, sing songs to him, follow him, sacrifice for him, do his will, run your race for him, put on his armor, and never turn from him.

GOOD DEEDS

Believers should live honorably, do what is right and good, and let their good deeds shine. They should also do them in private.

HEAVEN FOCUSED

Believers are to focus on the eternal place of rest, take the straight path, live as citizens of Heaven, and store their treasures in Heaven. If they can hold on to the end, they will eat fruit from the tree of life, drink the water of life, and receive Manna and a new name.

HOLY SPIRIT

A believer must receive the Holy Spirit but not smother the Holy Spirit. The Holy Spirit helps to ignite believer's hearts with passion to win non-believers to Christ.

HUSBANDS/WIVES/MEN/WOMEN

Many things are required here, but the recurring theme is that husbands and wives should submit to each other, especially to avoid immorality, and older and younger men and women have guidelines to follow.

IDOLATRY

Avoid idolatry, which is anything that comes before God and replaces the one, true God.

ILLNESS

Call the elders of the church to pray over the sick and anoint them with oil in the name of the Lord. And the prayer offered in faith will make the sick person well.

JESUS

Believers must follow Jesus, and many verses refer to this. It begins by taking up your cross and selling your possessions. Christians must live in and live like Jesus. They should stay true to Jesus, trust him, never be ashamed of him, worship him, believe in him, keep their eyes on him, and represent him and themselves accordingly.

JUDGING

Believers should respect and not criticize and judge non-believers, remembering that God will judge them on what they do. Of course, they must judge and guide other believers to the right path.

JUSTICE/FIGHTING

Believers are to obey and submit to the government and authorities, try to settle their differences, use fair discipline, and show mercy to each other.

LAWS AND COMMANDMENTS/BIBLE

Jesus came to fulfill the law and commandments, and believers must remember his commands. Additionally, they must obey the authorities and laws and handle legal disputes. Christians should hold firmly to the word of God and truthful teaching, listen to the Spirit, and avoid Godless teaching.

LOVE/JOY/PEACE

Love is the highest goal of the believer. They are to love people with brotherly affection, peace, compassion, harmony, and kindness. Christians motivate others to live with love and kindness, and we are to love other believers. Love is what he commanded believers to do.

MATERIAL POSSESSIONS

Believers are not to worry about food, clothes, or worldly desires; in fact, Christians should sell their possessions and follow Jesus.

MONEY

Believers understand that money is used to help others, especially through tithing. Givers should be cheerful and share with both God and the government. Money is the root of all evil, so believers must avoid greed and extortion, remembering the rich will be humbled and made to weep and groan.

NEIGHBORS/PEOPLE

We are to love and respect and give to our neighbors, strengthen them, give to them, share our home with them, attend to their urgent needs, encourage them, share each other's troubles and problems and show no favoritism.

THE POOR

God honors the poor because these people will inherit the Kingdom of God. So believers should invite the poor in, use their resources to help them, sell their possessions, and give to the poor.

PRAYING

Believers are to pray constantly and be disciplined people of prayer, and God gives us examples of prayer. We are to believe and receive, pray with our hands lifted through hardships, pray for sinners, and give our worries to God.

SALVATION

Believers are to become new persons, be baptized, cleanse themselves, receive the Holy Spirit, and live in the light. Believers must fight the good fight, work hard to enter God's Kingdom, and hold onto salvation to be victorious.

SECOND COMING

Believers are not to be fooled by those who say they know the Lord's return since no one knows those dates. However, we know the time is near, and Christians are to patiently wait, keep watch, and stay alert until then.

SERVANTS/GENEROSITY

Believers must understand that the most incredible people are servants to everyone. They help others with their urgent needs, give to others, share their homes, and even wash their feet.

SEX

Believers are to abstain from sexual immorality and sexual sin and run from lust and evil thoughts.

SINS/REPENTING

Believers must prove they have repented from sin by how they live and are to confess their sins to each other. God never tempts anyone to sin, and sin loses its power when they suffer for Jesus. Christians must stop, rebuke, avoid, turn from, repent, not tolerate, and deaden themselves to sin.

SUFFERING/TROUBLES

Believers must be glad when persecuted or endure suffering for Jesus, and God will reward them if they do. Even enslaved people should show full respect, obey, and endure for God.

TEACHING/LEARNING

Believers must open their hearts and grow in spiritual knowledge, listen and obey, and be faithful to teaching. They must also avoid human thinking and strange ideas, follow what is good, true, and pure, and be guided by the Holy Spirit. They must be of one mind, craving spiritual milk and following what is good. They must obey spiritual leaders, hold tightly to what they have, and defend their faith and the truth, remembering that wholesome teaching promotes a Godly life.

TEACHING (FALSE)

Believers are to stay away from anything that replaces God, including false teachers, false prophets, Pharisees, and wicked people who try to fool you and mock the truth or encourage idol worship.

WISDOM

Believers must be wise, understand true wisdom, and always seek wisdom.

SECTION FIVE

SIMPLE STEPS TO FOLLOWING GOD

SIMPLE STEPS TO FOLLOWING GOD

1 – God gave you Jesus to help you because he Loves You.

"God so loved the world that He gave His one and only Son, [Jesus), that whoever believes in Him shall not perish, but have eternal life" (John 3:16).

Jesus said, "I have come so that they may have life and have it abundantly." (John 10:10).

2 – The Issue: People are Sinful and Separated from God.

The Bible says, "All have sinned and fallen short of the glory of God." (Romans 3:23). Sin results in death and spiritual separation from God (Romans 6:23).

3 – Jesus Died for your Sins

"But God showed his great love for us by sending Christ to die for us while we were still sinners." (Romans 5:8). "Christ died for our sins, just as the Scriptures said. He was buried and raised from the dead on the third day." (1 Corinthians 15:3-4). Jesus is the only way to God. Jesus said, "I am the way, the truth, and the life. No one can come to the Father except through me. (John 14:6).

4 – The Good News: How to receive God's Forgiveness

1. Understand there is nothing we can do to earn salvation.
2. We are saved by God's grace when we have faith in His Son, Jesus Christ.
3. Believe you are a sinner, that Christ died for your sins, and ask His forgiveness.
4. Turn from your sins—which is called repentance.

SECTION SIX

HELPFUL PRAYERS TO TURN YOUR LIFE OVER TO GOD

HELPFUL PRAYERS TO TURN YOUR LIFE OVER TO GOD

"God, I know I am a sinner and ask for your forgiveness. I believe your son Jesus Christ died on the cross for my sins and rose again as my Savior. I will follow him from this day forward. Help me do your will and guide my life. In the name of Jesus, I pray, Amen."

"Lord Jesus, I believe you died for my sins so that I could be forgiven. I receive you, Jesus, as my Lord and Savior. Help me to do your will, and thank you for coming into my life. Amen."

SECTION SEVEN

GROWING IN JESUS CHRIST DAILY

GROWING IN JESUS CHRIST DAILY

ALWAYS REMEMBER the FRUITS of the SPIRIT

1. Love
2. Joy
3. Peace
4. Patience
5. Kindness
6. Goodness
7. Faithfulness
8. Gentleness
9. Self-control

BEWARE OF THE WARNING SIGNS OF FALLING AWAY FROM GOD

1. Regression (Backsliding or relapsing into bad behavior away from God).
2. Repression (Secret sin, or sin hidden from your neighbor).
3. Suppression (Bored with following Jesus or God).
4. Depression (No Joy in Following Jesus or God).
5. Oppression (Sin begins to manifest in your life).
6. Obsession (Reoccurring thoughts leading to sin).
7. Possession (Sin has taken full control over your life).
8. Death: (Spiritual, Mental, and Physical).

ABOUT THE AUTHOR

Kevin M. Thomas is an award-winning author of many books, including *Tao Te Ching De-Coded*, *Why Daughters Need Their Dads*, *Wisdom and Virtue*, *The Great Path*, *Chinese Spiritual Thoughts*, *The Happiest Women*, *Living the Life of Proverbs and Commands of the New Testament*. He has a varied background in Medicine, Alternative Health, Counseling, Religion, and Mind-Body Healing and is an Ordained Deacon Minister.

Kevin is passionate about promoting and delivering positive change to anyone. He strives to effect personal growth in individuals via Mind-Body-Spirit research and application. Finally, he considers his spiritual relationship with God and unconditional love for his children, Isiah, Caroline, Kimberly, Cheyenne, and the rest of his supportive family, including Erik, his most fabulous treasures.

BOOK SUMMARY

Commands of the New Testament is a tremendous reference and resource book for those who want to follow God's direction for their life.

Christians are saved by putting their faith in *Jesus Christ*, who lived a perfect life, *died* on the *cross* to pay for their *sins*, and rose again. God loves, forgives, and saves us not because of who we are or what we do but because of the work of Christ.

However, we cannot live as we please and follow God. The Bible says that we show our love for Jesus by obeying Him in all things: "If you love Me, keep My commandments" John 14:15

It is not enough to claim knowledge Of God; our actions must align with His teachings. Those who profess to know God but do not obey his commands are liars, deceiving themselves, and there is no truth in them. In contrast, all those who faithfully follow his word demonstrate a love for God that is genuine and complete. 1 John 2:3-11

Therefore, this book is about learning the Commands of the New Testament to fulfill God's wishes.

ABOUT KETNA PUBLISHING

Kevin Thomas and Erik Naugle own KETNA Publishing, a small hometown publisher in mid-Michigan. They aim to deliver high-quality information so people can positively change their lives by applying principles of body, mind, and spirit.

You can contact KETNA Publishing at grobthom@aol.com or write to KETNA Publishing, P.O. Box 90861, Burton, Michigan, 48509.

www.ingramcontent.com/pod-product-compliance
Lightning Source LLC
Chambersburg PA
CBHW070043080526
44586CB00013B/899